DIVINE SPARKS

DIVINE SPARKS

Messages To Inflame The Divine Spark Within

SHELIA SHUMATE

REVISED EDITION

COVER ART BY SIN D. PAINTEK

ISBN 0-9655078-1-5

LCCN 00-136337

WINDSONG PUBLISHING CO.

P.O. BOX 21005

SEDONA, AZ 86341

Dedication

I dedicate this book to all those who are opening their hearts, minds and souls to a greater awareness of what is.

The information presented in this book was created through inspirational thoughts and is designed to help guide and assist us on our earthly journey.

Shelia Shumate
Sedona, Arizona

ACKNOWLEDGMENTS

I wish to express my love and gratitude to the angels, guides and the Divine, who inspired and assisted me along my path.

I wish to express my love and gratitude to the many individuals who have attended my workshops and seminars, and to all my clients seeking guidance and greater awareness of self.

I wish to express love and gratitude to my children: Cheryl, Brian, Elaine and Roderick for their encouraging, nurturing and loving support.

I wish to thank my mentor and friend, George Addair, for his wisdom and truth.

I wish to thank all my friends, too numerous to mention, and my family. Each person is a very special gift that I cherish, and I wish to express my love, joy and gratitude.

PREFACE

Divine Sparks are 126 inspirational and insightful messages that came to me over a period of three consecutive nights. My guidance (Higher Self) said they were to be used in my readings, and were also for others to have and read. Each message is designed to bring an awareness of self, to encourage self, to inspire self, and to remember self.

I have received numerous letters and phone calls reporting great success with the *Divine Sparks* messages. Many people have enjoyed, been inspired by, grown and learned from them.

Recently, my guidance has encouraged me to put these messages in a book. They may be used for a "Reading" or for help with any question you may have. Think about what you want clarity on, such as your career, a relationship, or your spiritual path. Then randomly open the book and read the page your eyes rest on. Allow the message to speak to you. Repeat this process, if needed, for greater clarity.

Remember, there are no accidents. The messages you open to are perfect for you. To grow in consciousness is to be aware of yourself and these messages will help you to do that. Because of your own individuality, each message will provide what is best for you to hear, see, feel, or experience. No two people will interpret any message the same.

It gives me great pleasure to bring this information to you. It is an opportunity for you to help yourself by listening to your own inner voice. May you have fun, enjoy, and grow in consciousness!

TABLE OF CONTENTS

DIVINE SPARKS CARDS

TABLE OF CONTENTS

TABLE OF CONTENTS

TABLE OF CONTENTS

TABLE OF CONTENTS

TABLE OF CONTENTS

DIVINE

SPARKS

MESSAGES

ABUNDANCE is Yours. Know It! Believe It!

What a great word: abundance! Abundance is a plentiful supply. Abundance is not necessarily money or wealth. Abundance is about quantity. What do you desire an abundance of? An abundance of friendships, abundance of success, or abundance of water or land?

This message is a reminder that there is an unlimited supply of all things. What would it feel like for you to be abundant? Imagine it. What would you do if you were abundant in all things? Would you treat others any differently than you do now? Have you ever thought what choices you would make if a large sum of money landed in your lap? Perhaps you would buy houses, cars, land, or take trips, but then what? Is there a higher purpose you could use the money for? Do you see yourself helping others and if so, in what way? Do you believe the universe is unlimited?

Your beliefs about abundance shape your life. Start creating a limitless supply within you. Think of all the objects, relationships and events you have in your life—then feel abundant. Feel you have more than enough and give away what you are not using. Share. Be grateful. Abundance is yours; feel it, know it and believe it.

Acknowledge Your Strengths, Talents and Abilities. PROCLAIM!

What are your greatest strengths? What are your talents and abilities? Take time right now and focus on your gifts and strengths. Visualize yourself using your natural or acquired abilities. Continue this image until you have generated wonderful feelings about yourself. See yourself in situations where you are using your abilities. How does it feel? What are you doing? How are others affected by your efficiency, knowledge and competence?

Once you can visualize and believe it, you can achieve it. *Choose* to use your intelligence, ingenuity and cleverness to create anything you desire. Recognize what is within you, honor it and give thanks. Announce to the world that you are creating through your thoughts, words, actions and deeds.

To proclaim means to reveal, declare and make plain. Each of us have courage, will power and creativity within. How do you use yours? Throughout the day observe what you do to acknowledge your strengths. Life is your gift from the universe; you can choose to give back by using all your strengths, talents and abilities for the highest good of the world.

> **Align with Higher Self.**
>
> **BE OPEN.**
>
> LISTEN.

Many times there are messages from the Divine but we are not open to hear, see or know because we are out of balance, too busy or don't care. Ask yourself, "Do I want my life to flow? Do I want happiness? Do I want beautiful relationships? Do I want abundance? Do I want peace?" If so, then connect with your inner guidance.

How do you connect with inner guidance? First of all, state your desire to connect. Make a conscious choice to be aligned with your Higher Self. Relax your body, close your eyes and feel your breath. Know you have the answers within. Be open, be still and listen. Are you out of balance? Are you in judgment about yourself? Think positively. We can receive messages at any given moment. If we are stressed, unbalanced and in fear it is difficult to hear and understand.

Think of a radio and how it receives information across the air waves. Imagine yourself being a receiver for information from the spirit world. Be open and aware. You can switch the station on and listen. You can tune into your guidance. Align with Higher Self through stillness. It may take some adjustment and fine-tuning of your receiver, but what a great station to listen to: **Divine Guidance!**

ALLOW CREATIVITY TO FLOW THROUGH YOU!

Are you allowing something original, imaginative and ingenious to stream forth? If you open yourself to all possibilities, your thoughts and actions will be different. Acknowledge yourself as creative.

Remember, being creative doesn't necessarily just mean painting, writing or sculpting. What about being creative in the way you approach customers, creative in making your reports, creative in business meetings, creative in ministering, creative in cooking, or creative in warming the hearts of others?

When you are creative, you are resourceful. When you are resourceful, you are clever. When you are clever, you are intelligent. When you are intelligent, you are perceptive. When you are perceptive, you are observant. When you are observant, you are being aware of the moment. In that moment you can *choose* to allow the creativity to flow through you.

It is so wonderful to know we are unlimited in our creativity. Whatever the mind can conceive and believe, it can achieve. Trust your creative side and watch it grow. Allow the flow.

> **Allow Spirit to Help. Flow. Release and let go.**

No matter what situation you find yourself in, no matter what emotional state you're in, no matter what state of health you're in, you have the *choice* today to begin anew. Think differently. Feel differently. Ask for help and be willing to receive. Each moment in time is a moment to be aware of what you are creating.

Do you want guidance from spirit? Ask for it. Spirit is always ready to assist. Sit still, get in touch with your breath and let go of all negative emotions and thoughts. Listen. Do not discount anything you hear or see within.

You are creating your reality moment by moment. Allow spirit to help. Be in the flow of life rather than pushing or struggling. Release what no longer serves you. How do you choose to live: in beauty and joy or in sadness and misery? Change your thinking and watch what happens to your life.

Any time during the day you become aware of negative situations, look for the positive and then turn it over to a higher power and allow the flow. Allow Spirit to put things in perspective. Go with the flow. Release and let go of negative thinking, events and people. Relax and watch the results of your action.

Allow the Wisdom of the Divine Guidance to fill your Essence Self.

Essence is the soul. Essence seeks the path of love. When you are aware of the physical body's connection to the Divine you will be guided. Your life will flow when you allow Divine Guidance to come into your awareness.

Today, take a moment and imagine what it would be like to be detached from outcomes in your life. What if you had no expectations of what tomorrow will bring? If this day was your last, what choices would you make? Would they be positive or negative? Would they be of regret or satisfaction? What if you turned every event in your life over to the Divine and you decided to have fun, stay in the moment and be in a space of love. Think of how that feels. What would it be like to be free of worry and fret? What would it feel like to be who you are and not put on an act for others?

Take time to relax and smile at everyone you meet. When you get up in the morning say a prayer of gratitude that you have been given another day to be present. Ask the Divine to lead you through all your activities and conversations. Allow the wisdom of the Divine to guide you with every step.

Allow Your PASSION to Awaken.

Do you know what you want from life? What is your passion? Is there a driving force to be an artist or actor? Do you have a hunger to spread your knowledge to others? Is there a need or cause calling you? Do you have excitement about healing others? What do you love? If your job or career does not satisfy you, then make a change.

Now is the time to allow your passion to awaken. Do what you love! Has your relationship lost its passion? If so, then what can you do to bring it back? If you're getting signs not to be in it any more, then make the choice to move on.

Each of us is born with a passion for something, which may take a long time to discover. Maybe you have always wanted to be a singer or minister but felt no support to do it. Call upon your guidance for support. As you explore your options you allow new beginnings. Open up. There is no stopping you when you allow your passion to awaken.

You can *choose* to be, achieve and create anything you desire. Know that opportunities to advance your relationships, career and spirit are there. Your life will become more fulfilling and joyful. Allow.

> **ASK and You Shall RECEIVE.**
>
> **SEEK and You Shall FIND.**
>
> **KNOCK and the Door shall OPEN.**

Request what you want; then release it to the Divine. Discover the power within yourself. When you put your thoughts, talents, skills and energy towards your vision, the universe will give you opportunities.

Do you ever wonder why some people always seem to be in the right place at the right time? They listen, observe and take action. When you ask for a particular thing, think about how many people the Divine touches in order for the perfect occasion to happen. Many people are involved and that is why the connection with spirit is extremely important.

Seek and you shall find. If you have true faith and are listening to Guidance, the results will be there for you, though the means to the end may not be as you think. Use your intuition and allow the knowingness to guide you. Knock and the door shall open.

'Knock' means it takes effort on your part to have something happen. Think about the desired result. Make phone calls, write letters, study or learn and before long the door will open. Remember, you must take the action to achieve the desired reaction.

**B
A
L
A
N
C
E**

What does balance mean to you? What does life look like when you are in balance? Imagine balance in your relationships, family, social settings, business and career. Take a moment before reading on and *feel* balance for yourself in all those situations.

Balance is a steadiness of body and emotions. It is a state of equilibrium. Balance is being in harmony with self. Whenever you act from a place of poise, level-headedness and composure, your **choices** will be for your best interest. Being in balance creates cooperation, unity, understanding and peace within. Do you desire balance in your life? What can you do today to create a state of balance? What would happen to the world if everyone was in balance? You can set the example.

Being aware of your composure and acting from it encourages others to find their balance. By using your inner power you make it easier for others to find theirs. The more you're in harmony and peace, the more you inspire others to be in harmony and peace.

When you help yourself, mankind benefits. When you help others, society benefits. Become aware that everything you do makes a difference in the world.

BECOME AWARE of your feeling at this moment. **GIVE THANKS.**

What impressions have you been receiving? Are you highly emotional? Do you respond with compassion or judgment? Are your feelings ones of sadness, anger, frustration or appreciation? Be in touch with what is going on within you and identify the emotions. Then ask yourself, "What does this say to me about me? What is the bigger picture here? What do I have to be thankful for?" Look at all the viewpoints, consider what is worthy and be grateful for any insight.

If you have a 'gut feeling', an intuition or just a knowing, then act upon that. Give thanks for it. To acknowledge it strengthens the bond between you and your guidance. Guidance is there every step and season of your life. Life is developing at this time into something greater than you're even aware of. Know you are advancing—advancing towards love.

Become aware of your feelings and see where you are at this moment. Are you being negative or positive? In order to be different we must think differently and feel differently. Remember, you have a *choice* to view life from a different perspective. Find something to be grateful for in all situations and people.

When you become filled with too many thoughts, opinions, beliefs and judgments, it is difficult to bring in anything new. Think of a glass full of juice and you want to taste water. What happens when you pour some water into a full glass of juice? Are you able to experience what pure water tastes like? The same is true with your mind; it is full of past experiences that dilute the new ones you're having.

Is it time for a change? Is it a time to let go of past experiences, beliefs and opinions? Let go of what doesn't feel right for you. It could be lack of self esteem, a career that's not satisfying, a relationship that is not supportive, a religious upbringing that no longer fits, or so many other things. You have outgrown something that served you in the past. You are growing, seeing and experiencing life in a different way. Acknowledge it. Believe it. Celebrate it. Claim it.

Know you are becoming new, just as a caterpillar changes and becomes a butterfly. You must let go of the old in order to bring in the new. Discard what doesn't fit and you will be delighted. Be thankful for what is coming. Allow. Become empty of old thoughts, beliefs and patterns and fill yourself with the new.

BE COMMITTED TO YOUR OWN EVOLUTION.

Is your life hectic? Often people say they do not have enough time for themselves. However, when you do not *choose* to take time for yourself you may become confused, overwhelmed or scattered, and then place the blame on others. Ask yourself, "Am I committed to my own evolution? Do I allow time for myself to relax, read or meditate?"

What is commitment to you? Do you have the commitment to follow the path to higher evolution? Have you accepted responsibility for your own consciousness? Start by making a pledge to yourself to take 10-15 minutes each day for spiritual growth. Concentrate on your breathing, give silent gratitude or just become aware of your thoughts and behavior. What takes priority in your life? Are you in balance with work, play, social life, family and spirit?

You are more than this physical body; you are a spiritual being in a human form. You evolve as you open up your intuition and awareness. Listen to the voice within and see what is best for you. Relax your body, take a walk in nature, read inspirational material or concentrate on your breathing. To be committed to your own evolution takes effort and deliberation.

Be in
HARMONY
with all
parts of
self.
ACCEPT.

When you are in harmony with all parts of self, you are in balance. When you are in balance you can have a greater understanding of situations and others. If your emotions are out of balance, it is difficult to hear your inner voice; therefore, stress arises. As you learn to accept your emotions, feelings and thoughts, you achieve calmness.

As a child your beliefs about life were formed by adults: what is good, what is bad, what is right, what is wrong. Now that you are an adult, you can choose to accept yourself and be in harmony with all parts of you. At the first signs of not accepting yourself, situations or family members, look at the belief behind it. What's happening? Are you giving your power away? Do you want approval? Are you wanting to be perfect? By asking yourself questions, you gain insight about who you are, and the truth will surface.

What viewpoints have you not explored about a situation or yourself? What can you do in this moment to accept yourself as you are: your body, your mind, your thoughts, your emotions and your actions? Accepting **you**, as you are, allows for the betterment of self. See yourself in harmony and love. Accept and enjoy this moment.

> **Believe in Yourself.**
> **You are more than just this Physical Body.**

When you begin to see the greatness beyond the physical body you will notice the value of self increases. Imagine the physical body as a shell, like an oyster. When you open it there is a pearl inside, which is beautiful and very valuable. Within our physical body is a soul, like the pearl, which is beautiful and very valuable. The pearl is created from debris irritation in the oyster. On this Earth plane we are faced with irritations and negativity and through our trials we grow and learn. Our soul increases in consciousness, which is valuable. The soul is our essence that lives on after the physical body dies.

In this lifetime you are given an opportunity to raise the vibration of your soul. Therefore, you may be given many chances to believe in yourself. You may be given many chances to trust in your guidance. You may be given many chances to have faith in your abilities. Trust that all is in Divine order.

As you know, you are more than just this physical body. Believe in who you truly are: a spiritual light-being full of love, beauty and joy. Remember, you are physical, emotional, mental and spiritual energies working together. Believe in yourself!

Believe in your VISION.

JOYFULLY AWAKE.

What is your vision? What do you love to do? Remember, whatever you can conceive and believe—you can achieve. What are you waiting for? Money, age, other people's approval or what? Are there old patterns and belief systems that hold you back?

Take a moment and tell yourself, "I am unlimited. There is an inexhaustible supply of funds from the universe. I can live abundantly. I am confident, my talents and skills are never ending. My angels and spirits are guiding me every step of the way. I can have a wonderful and caring relationship. The Divine is helping me to create positive situations for myself. I am focused and able to create the life I desire through my thoughts, words and actions." Do you believe that? How does it feel?

If you believe this, then your vision will happen. Say this over and over until you know what it feels like to be unlimited, to have an inexhaustible supply of funds, etc. Joyfully awaken to who you are. Be joyful in others' accomplishments. Feel grateful for and delight in your accomplishments. Believe in your vision. *Choose* to feel excited and blessed with the decisions you've made. Awaken to the joy within!

```
     B  e
  O  P  E  N
     t o
    N e w
Beginnings.
```

New beginnings are not always easy for people. However, beginnings can be exciting and fun. You are changing and learning so you have an opportunity to understand more of who you are and your spiritual self. Ask yourself, "Am I in trust or fear?" Fear is negative and negative brings gloom and reluctance. Reluctance brings a struggle and struggle brings on difficulties. Who wants difficulties in their life?

Trust is positive and positive brings understanding and acceptance. Acceptance brings gratification and gratification brings faith. Who wouldn't want faith in their life? Faith and trust are divine. Divine guidance is within reach; listen. Be open to new beginnings. Remember, you can *choose* to be open and allow life to unfold. As you open to changes there can be excitement and joy about the unknown.

Ask your angels and guides to be with you for comfort and assurance through the changes. Recall other times of new beginnings and feel that excitement and joy. Your attitude has so much to do with the results. Be open. Think positively and enjoy the adventure.

What would happen if you stopped breathing right now? Is every breath you take Divine? By becoming aware of each breath you take you can be fully present in the moment. Stop for a minute and become aware of your body. Is it tense or relaxed? Feel the rise and fall of your chest as you breathe. Become aware of the current of air going in and out. Pause and become aware again. If thoughts arise, just let them flow in and out of your mind, giving them no energy and go back to your breathing exercise. After you do this for several minutes, become aware of your body again. Does it feel heavy and tense or light and relaxed?

Each day brings social, legal or moral ties. You may have contracts and promises to fulfill; you could be hustling here and there without ever being aware of going from one activity to another. Life can become a big blur. If that is the case, take time to pause and become aware of your divine breath, and give thanks for this precious gift of life.

If you want your life to get better, do not take each day for granted. Start being grateful for what you have and begin to see positive results. Become aware of your breath and the Divine.

CELEBRATE WHO YOU ARE. ACCEPT SELF & OTHERS. LOVE ALL PARTS OF YOURSELF.

We celebrate our birthdays and holidays, but what if every day was a celebration? What if you decided to put aside some time to rejoice in who you are, to respect who you are, to praise and honor who you are? Many of our thoughts are filled with criticism or ridicule about who we are, but that's a choice we make.

Take a moment and allow thoughts of excitement and gratitude to surface. If you first accept yourself, you are more willing to accept others. What trait or behavior do you not like in yourself? Imagine loving and accepting it.

Life can be fun and festive when we celebrate and accept who we are. If thoughts of fault-finding appear, turn them into ones of acceptance and love. If you feel tenderness within, it shows in your actions. If you feel beauty inside, it shows in your words and deeds. Focus on your assets.

Do you know your strengths, talents and abilities? Understand who you are through observation of your traits and behavior so you can celebrate them. Each of us are unique and special in our own way. Observe how you treat yourself and others. Celebrate who you are!

CHOOSE LOVE.

FORGIVE.

We can only feel one emotion at a time. At any given moment you choose to feel love or choose to feel hate. Love is positive, hate is negative. Love is beauty, hate is ugly. Love is affection, hate is hostility. Love is admiration, hate is disdain. Love is respect, hate is disrespect. Love is devotion, hate is betrayal. Love is tender, hate is harsh. Love is harmony, hate is spiteful. Love is understanding, hate is antipathy. Love is rejoicing, hate is destruction. Choose love.

Who could you forgive today? An old flame that you felt mislead you, a family member that dominated you, a friend who lied to you, an angry co-worker, a boss that denied your promotion, or yourself for your own words and actions? You can stop feeling anger and resentment by giving it up, letting it go, then choosing love and forgiving.

See how other people helped you to be who you are today. Learn from the experiences and see the valuable lessons. Allow your thoughts and energy to be used for betterment of self, and forgive past negative experiences. You can *choose* love today through forgiveness.

Claim Your Power. *FORTITUDE* Know Who You Are.

Power is the ability to use your strength and courage no matter what you are faced with. Fortitude is the strength of mind that allows you to endure pain or adversity with courage. Get in touch with your inner power and strength.

As of this moment start observing your actions, your habits, your thoughts and your words without judgment. Through observation you learn your strengths and weaknesses; then in turn you will make choices that are best for you. You will be able to claim the power within you and know who you are from moment to moment.

Are you using your strength now or are you feeling weak? To be aware of who you are in the moment helps to call upon power and fortitude. Become aware of the moment rather than unconsciously going from one activity to another. Doing so will put you in touch with your power, moral strength, patience and endurance. This helps to bring balance in the moment.

Throughout the day ask yourself, "Am I aware of this moment? Am I acting or reacting from automatic behavior?" In that moment you can claim your power by observing self.

CLEAR YOUR HEAD. FEEL Your FEELINGS.

When your mind is full of chatter, it is very difficult to feel your feelings. Sit quietly and do not give energy to the thoughts you have at this time. Allow them to float into your head and out. Be aware of them, then let go of frustrations, blame, worry or guilt, and free yourself from confusion. Also, observe your thoughts and identify them. If a thought from the past arises, say *past*; if it's a thought about the future, say *future*; if it's about this moment, say *present*. Then give yourself a *present* by living in the moment.

You can change your thoughts by identifying them and then not dwelling on them. Thoughts are energy. You spend energy when you reflect on a situation over and over. What a drain on your body! What is the purpose? To resolve, to relive, to regret, to calculate or to judge? Ask yourself, "How does it serve me in this moment?" Release those thoughts and quiet the mind.

Get in touch with your emotions. Are they negative or positive? Choose the state of mind you want. The past is over; enjoy your *present* of today. Clear your head of mind chatter and be in touch with what you're feeling. Use your energy wisely, keep your mind in this moment, experience your feelings and enjoy.

CONFRONT The Belief Systems That Limit You!

Are you ready to face your convictions and your opinions? Are you ready to see if they fit for you anymore? Could they be outdated? Do you truly believe in them, or have them only because your parents, teachers, religion or society says that is the way to think?

To know your truth, you must quiet the mind, get in touch with your breath, then go within and allow your feelings to surface. What are your beliefs about spirituality and religion? What are your beliefs about listening to inner guidance? What are your beliefs about medical healing versus mind/body healing? What are your beliefs about being in total control versus letting it flow? What are your beliefs about the existence of angels and spirit guides? Do you believe in miracles? Do you believe you are unlimited?

As a child you were taught what others believed about life. As a child you were very impressionable, and you took that on as your truth and may still be using someone else's views and opinions. Today, give thought about your beliefs and journal how you feel about life. Confront the belief systems that limit you! It can be very rewarding and rejuvenating.

CONNECT with Nature & Bring LIGHT to Self.

Mother earth has a wonderful way of showing us her beauty: sunsets, forests, lakes, mountains, oceans, and beaches. Nature is inspiring and wondrous if we allow ourselves the experience. When we take the time to become one with nature, it changes our outlook. Think of a time when you were sitting or walking in nature. Remember the sights and sounds? How did that feel?

Nature is a place of beauty. Beauty brings calmness. Calmness brings relaxation. Relaxation brings silence. Silence connects you with your guidance. Guidance brings insight. When you connect with nature and all its beauty, your energy will change. It is your experience and no one can tell you what will happen because each of us will have a different adventure.

Today, go for a walk or sit in nature and be one with it. If time does not allow this, then take an object such as a flower, rock or leaf and focus on it, seeing, feeling and being it. What changes occur for you while being one with nature? Connect with your house plants, trees, clouds and sky. You have the opportunity to bring light to yourself through nature.

CONNECT with Your Spirit Guides. BE ATTENTIVE.

Do you want to increase your awareness? Do you want guidance in all that you do? If the answers are yes, you must *choose* to listen. How do you do that? Several different ways. Do any or all of these and see which one works best for you: (1) Sit quietly and concentrate on your breath, allowing thoughts to come and go without giving them energy. (2) Observe in nature using your five senses; become one with your surroundings. (3) Hold an object and ask questions such as: Who made you? Where did you come from? Why are you here? What is your message for me? etc. (4) When you get hunches, gut feelings or knowingness, at that time *give thanks* for the connection. This will strengthen the bond between lower and Higher Self.

Any of these will help to merge guidance into your awareness. Be aware of any thoughts, feelings or images that appear to you while doing them. See how they relate in your life. Connecting as often as possible will strengthen your relationship with *Spirit.* You must listen and be watchful. Listen to the wind, birds, trees and animals; Spirit is there. Give thanks when you have connected with your guides.

This is a time for you to do something original—a time to use your talents and abilities in a most wonderful way. Create can invent. Create can mold. Create can construct. Create can devise. Create can formulate. Create can form. Create can conceive. Create can fashion. Create sows the seeds. Create can establish. Create is giving birth to an idea. Create is taking action for the idea to be in physical form. Create is having the idea manifested.

You can *choose* to use your gifts and expertise to create something of beauty. Beauty is within you, waiting to be made visible. Uncover your hidden artistic potential. Demonstrate through illustration. Make known that which is in your imagination. Express yourself verbally. Bring yourself to the light. Of course, you can delay, procrastinate and block your ingenuity, or you can do something constructive.

You are the creator of your reality. Do you want to use your creativity in a most positive way? Listen to the voice within and know opportunities await. *Choose* to have fun and create. Create whatever you desire.

DISCOVER
YOUR
GREATNESS.
Feel Love and
Confidence.

Within you is an abundance of Divine Love, power, strength and confidence. Do you believe it? Do your thoughts and actions show it? The deep inner knowing believes it but the human part may have doubts and fears. There may be questions of: What if? Should I? Could I? and other thoughts that prevent you from being your greatest.

You can begin today to make decisions that raise your confidence. Close your eyes and visualize yourself feeling confident, significant and important. Take that feeling and put it into a situation where you lack confidence. See all the details in your mind. Feel strength, courage, confidence and love, then draw upon these feelings whenever needed. If you are critical of others, that is negativity. The negative goes out into the universe bringing back negative to you. You are a magnet to the world. What you put out comes back to you.

Your thoughts and actions create your tomorrow. Think thoughts of greatness. Focus on your strengths and talents. Discover your greatness. Be confident. If you feel unworthy, then unworthy goes out into the universe and brings back unworthy to you. *Choose* your thoughts with care. Discover your greatness. Feel love and confidence.

**Practice
Faith & Trust.**

Faith cannot be seen. Trust is not tangible. How does one practice something they cannot see or touch? Deep within you there is a guiding force, a magnificent sense of cosmic bliss. A place where you are radiant and glorified. A place of lightness and joy. That place is Divine. Divine works in your life. Even though you may not be aware of its presence, it is there. It is working for your highest good.

When you *choose* to acknowledge the presence of Divine, your life takes a turn in the most wonderful way. This doesn't mean you will not have any difficulties; instead your troubles and obstacles will be handled with less stress and more relaxation, less irritability and more loving, less complication and more flowing, less confusion and more understanding, less oppressiveness and more freedom. Become aware of your decisions.

How do you make your decisions? Is it from intuition or your head? With intuition you 'just know'. There may be no facts to back it up, and society, friends and family may not agree. Your head says, "This is best," with facts and data to justify. The *choice* is yours; practice faith and trust with your inner voice.

DIVINE GUIDANCE is at Hand.

LISTEN.

What does holy mean to you? What does the word sacred mean? Do these terms feel religious or spiritual? Is Divine heavenly? Is Divine excellence? Is Divine wonderful? Is Divine God, Goddess, All-That-Is, Higher Self or Universal Mind? Within you is a higher power, a spirit, a soul and a guidance that wants you to be all you can be.

The key is to listen. Listening opens the doors of opportunity. You can be in the right place at the right time and dreams will come true. The Divine wants you to be happy, successful and prosperous.

Do you ever wonder why you don't listen to the quiet voice, intuition or knowingness? You have been taught from childhood what your parents believed to be the truth; what is real, tangible and factual. You have lived in a world of comparisons: good-bad, right-wrong about religious beliefs, political preference, skin colors, education, people, manners and more. Your mind is full of those thoughts and beliefs. Yet also within is Divine guidance, a *knowingness*.

Choose to become still. Stop the mind chatter, quiet the emotions, become present and listen. Deep within you, know guidance is at hand. Trust that.

Do Not Be Critical of Self. ACCEPT, ALLOW, & FORGIVE.

Do you judge or find fault in yourself constantly? Observe yourself today and see if you are giving yourself permission to be who you are. No matter what you have done, created or said in the past, it is over. You cannot change it so leave it behind. Do not give it any more thought or energy. Forgive yourself.

Now is the time to move forward with loving thoughts about yourself. Think of your past as a learning experience and not as right or wrong, good or bad. It just was. It was an opportunity to know yourself.

Through those experiences you learned valuable lessons about the power within you, your courage, your determination, your intensity, your balance, your resistance and so on. You had those experiences; now instead of reliving them through your thoughts and feelings, *choose* a different experience by being present today, and see what valuable insight comes.

As you begin to forgive yourself and others, you will stop finding fault or reliving a past injury. Accept who you are. Stop being in anger, resentment and negativity. If you want the most out of life, live it by being present and aware. Allow. Whenever you notice yourself being critical, turn it over to the Divine and *choose* love. Accept and forgive yourself and others; allow life to unfold.

> **DO NOT LIMIT SELF. Your VIEW of Reality is not the ONLY ONE.**

Where are your boundaries? What is the farthest you will go to create what you desire? Will you extend yourself beyond what you believe? Is what you believe what your parents believed? Were beliefs passed down to you and now you do not question them? When you see another's point of view without judgment, that enhances you.

When you *choose* to listen to other people's beliefs, opinions and thoughts without judgment, that's a higher way of living. You can improve your life by living without limitations and restrictions. How can you change your behavior? How you react to every situation reveals your true nature. Remember, how others think, act and speak are based upon their past hurts and pain. Keep in mind they are who they are. Accept them. Watch yourself and understand why you act or react.

Imagine a wagon wheel, a circle within a circle. The center circle is Source, God, Universal Mind and The Divine, and the outer circle is life. Each spoke is a path back to Source. Each path is different, as each of us have different realities. We limit ourselves when we think our path is the only way. Live unlimited. Open up and understand others.

Where are you *choosing* to limit yourself? You have strength, talents and abilities to do whatever you desire. If you can conceive it and believe it, you can achieve it.

Remember: *Limit binds—unlimited is boundless. Limit determines—unlimited is open. Limit is measurable—unlimited is vast. Limit has an end—unlimited is endless. Limit sets a figure—unlimited is numberless.*

You are unlimited and inexhaustible. There are endless possibilities. Take a moment and ask yourself, "What would I be doing if I knew I was without limitations?" You have all the money, skills and talents necessary to do whatever you desire. What would it feel like to be financially independent? In balance? In a loving and caring relationship? Successful in your business career? Being connected to your higher guidance?

You can *choose* to create this for yourself through your thoughts, words, deeds, emotions and actions. Every time you hear a voice in your head about limitations, stop and change it to one of being unlimited; then feel love and confidence. Listen and know you are being guided in a most wonderful way.

Do What Gives You JOY. *EXPRESS BEAUTY.*

What do you desire to be: a musician, a lecturer, an artist, a store owner, an entrepreneur, a lover or a social worker? No matter what you are dreaming of, you can achieve it. Do not let age, sex, skin color or anything else get in the way of achieving. Express beauty through joy.

Today, take the first step: create a plan, make a phone call, sign up for a class, read a book, meditate, talk with a successful person who's doing what you desire and so on. If you have hesitation about anything in your life right now, ask why. What holds you back? Fear of the unknown, of making a mistake, of failing or that love might not last forever? Today is all you have; tomorrow might not ever come for you. Take the risk. Move into the unknown and explore. Find the beauty and do what gives you joy. Enjoy. Savor the moment. If you make a mistake, learn from it. Maybe love won't last a lifetime, but if you don't love now, when? Let go of any thoughts that stop you from achieving what you desire.

You are creating your reality at this very moment. What would give you joy? Do it! The beauty of expression will come though. Know within you is beauty. Know within you is joy.

Do You Find Yourself Reacting to Situations or Choosing to Act?

If you notice that you are reacting instead of choosing to act, become aware of why. Are you reacting from past experiences? Reacting from habit? Reacting from an attachment to an outcome? Reacting from wanting to be in control? Once you become aware of why you are reacting, then changes can begin.

The next time you become aware of wanting it your way, not listening, emotions out of balance or reacting from habit, stop and observe yourself and others. Listen to their viewpoints. Understand why they think, feel and act that way. See the whole picture of what is happening, then consciously choose to act. Do you react to situations, and later think "I could have," or "I should have," or "what if I had?" Stop those thoughts. It happened. It is already in the past. *Choose* to let it go.

What can you do today to be more aware of your thoughts, words and actions? Observe yourself and learn from what you do and who you are. Are you balanced? If not, you may be reacting from emotions. Are you tense and overwhelmed? If so, you may be reacting from stress. By observing where you are now, you can consciously make decisions that will help for the next moment in time. Be conscious and choose to act!

Draw upon your
Courage and
Strength NOW.
Use Will Power.

Can you face a new situation or difficulty with total confidence? Within you is the courage and strength to overcome any obstacle. Use your willpower to create or accomplish what you desire. You can do it. You can overcome or change anything in your life.

You are a spiritual being, so call upon your guidance. Know you are powerful and ready to tackle anything. Be self-assured and trust in higher guidance. Within you is all the willpower you need. Concentration is an important factor for using willpower. Hold the focus on what you desire, for this strengthens the will to see it through. Do not waste time and energy on negative supposition; that will drain you and keep you from using will and effort.

What you give attention to, flows to you. Know what you want. Use your courage, strength and willpower. Life flows easier when you focus on the positive. Don't worry over details, leave that to Spirit. Listen and get in touch with what feels best. Feel accomplishment, vitality and determination. You have the courage and strength; use it.

ENERGY Follows Thought. What are You giving Energy to?

When you are thinking about the past or worried about the future, you drain yourself of valuable energy. You may feel sluggish, tired or even exhausted from spending a day being worried. Think of a time when you were anxious, disturbed or troubled and recall your energy level.

When you keep thinking the same thoughts about the same situation, or the same person, your body is using precious energy and you are giving your power away. **STOP.** Focus on what is at hand. What are you doing? Start visualizing positive results. Enjoy the moment. Feel delighted and be cheerful. Sing a song that uplifts you. Do something that elevates you emotionally and spiritually. Use your energy wisely and you will become happier and more energized.

You have the power to concentrate. Concentrate on what is positive. Positive thinking produces positive results. Become aware of your energy level at this time. Is it where you want it to be? If not, imagine how you want to feel, to think and to be. Where are you putting your energy? Each situation is an opportunity to become aware of your thoughts, behavior and energy.

Everything that Happens is Teaching YOU Something.

What if every person you meet and every situation you find yourself in is really an opportunity to learn about who you are? How would that make you feel? Think of every relationship you have ever had: each has been a lesson. Think of relationships you have been in with relatives, friends, bosses, employees or lovers and get in touch with what you have learned from them, such as strength, respect, boldness, warmth, intensity, persistence or honor. Then give thanks for the experience you had with them. At this point you can create a different attitude about yourself and others.

Everything that happens is teaching you something. Let's say you are in a relationship and the other person doesn't value your opinions. Maybe you are learning how to value your own opinions, or how to set boundaries, or how to respect yourself. If a situation arises where you feel weak, this might be an opportunity to have faith and trust and draw upon your inner strength. Everything that happens is teaching you something. Choose to see the gift and the lesson in the situation and learn from it. Come from a positive perspective and allow yourself to be uplifted.

EXPERIENCE an Expanded View of Truth. Others can be a REFLECTION for you. LOVE.

To experience an expanded view of truth, first know your viewpoint and then be open to hear and understand what others say. Understanding expands who you are. We are all part of the whole. Next time someone disagrees with you take a moment and put yourself in their shoes: why do they think that, what would it feel like to have their experiences, why do they act that way and say those things? Being aware of others can open your heart and allow a greater compassion for them.

Choose to love others. Others can reflect parts of yourself in their behavior. If there is a trait or behavior in others that annoys you, ask yourself, "What does this say to me about me?" Is it impatience, jealousy, selfishness, judgmentalness, independence or greed that you don't like? Now ask, "Am I like that?" If not, then ask, "Am I the opposite? Am I very giving but intolerant of selfish behavior in myself?" If so, accept that part of you. We all have two sides: strong-weak, giving-taking, loving-hateful. The other person is helping you to have a greater understanding of yourself. They are a gift; thank them. Love self and others.

FACE THE CHALLENGE AND RADIATE.

If you were called upon to use your talents, abilities, resources and energy to the fullest, what would be the result? When you are faced with a risk, an obstacle or a problem, remember, you can use all your strengths, your enthusiasm and your inner power to come out winning and full of joy. Remember the excitement you had when you accomplished a task that was extremely difficult? Face the challenge and radiate.

You can face any challenge. Observe your thoughts, actions and words. What are you saying to yourself: uplifting words of encouragement or words that are degrading and belittling? What would it feel like to radiate confidence and love? Feel it. How are others affected by your positive self and your negative self? Beliefs decide how we face situations. If you believe you will radiate, you will radiate. If you believe you can't do it, you won't be able to do it.

Next time you are confronted with frustrations, disagreements or problems, call upon your inner self; listen and know the appropriate action. Believe there is nothing you cannot accomplish because within you is the power to face any challenge and radiate!

FACE the Unfinished Business in Your Life. Heal, Release, and LOVE.

Directly confront that in your life which has not been resolved. What is still unfinished? Heal, release and love. Can you imagine how you want your future to be? Take responsibility for the life you desire through your thoughts, expressions and feats. Before deciding on your purpose and what you want to achieve, you must first take care of unfinished business. Unfinished business could be about anger, hurts and disappointments within family, relationships or career.

Where are you allowing your energy to be drained? What is unsettled within you? Take care of the unfinished business by making calls, writing letters, asking for guidance or releasing thoughts that no longer serve you. Heal by letting go and forgiving through love. Visualize a desired outcome. Quiet your mind and feel what is the best way to heal and release.

Ask your angels, guides and spirits to help you have the words and action necessary to create peace within. What would it feel like to be cleansed, released and healed and full of compassion, peace and joy? Today is an opportunity to go forth with love.

FACE YOUR FEARS. Feel It. Let Go.

Fear may arise when we don't understand something, or are unsure of where we are going. You can be in a space of love or in a space of fear. Fear arises from anything: fear of being alone, fear of health problems, fear of financial difficulties, etc. Do you believe in a greater power and intelligence than yourself? If so, then you know that power, the Divine, flows through you at all times. Open up to the wisdom it holds. Trust and know that it will be revealed.

Face your fears by asking yourself what's the worst that can happen, and then think about what you would do. Once there is a plan of action, the pressure is off. When a situation arises where you are in confusion or uncertainty about the outcome, take a deep breath and relax the body. Call upon your angels and spirits for guidance. Focus on a positive outcome, and know whatever decision you make will be the best. After the fear has been identified, be it fear of failure or success, fear of pain or hurt, or fear of being wrong, feel it and let it go. Move into a place of confidence. Trust and listen. Allow the Divine to work out the details.

**FEEL the
'I AM'
Presence.**

Are you whole and complete just as you are? Are you Divine? Close your eyes and visualize yourself being whole and complete. Feel Divine. How does it feel? What attitude do you present to the world? Are you limited? Are you in balance emotionally, mentally and physically? What are your thoughts? Stay with the image until you experience being Divine, complete and whole. When you are in touch with a higher vibration of energy, say, "I am that I am." Repeat it several times.

From now on, whenever you are going through something that is disturbing, emotional, painful or out of balance in any way, stop and remember to say, "I am that I am." Bring back the feelings you had in the visualization. Then say, "All is in a Divine plan. I am complete and whole just as I am." Repeating this phrase helps you to return to your center and connect with your Higher Self.

You are more than this physical body. You are light, love and Divinity. Just for today, choose positive thoughts and encouraging words. Just for today, choose uplifting feelings and harmonious actions. Just for today, choose to be complete and whole just as you are. Feel the I AM presence.

Finish what you Start. COMPLETION.

When you begin an activity and then leave without completing it, your energy remains in the project. What in your life has begun and not yet finished? Is it a project, a situation, or a relationship? If there is something not finished, make a decision to continue or end it. Remember, there is *power* in finishing projects, clearing up old relationships and saying what needs to be said. Not only is it empowering but it brings comfort and joy.

You are working on being whole and complete, so use your skills and abilities to finish what you start. Look at your past with love and acknowledge what you have learned from your experiences. Finish what you start. Each past situation has made you who you are today. Become aware of the moment you make a commitment and become aware when you no longer want to go that path; then end it and move forward.

We have more time to do what we want to do in this moment when we are not thinking of projects that haven't been completed. Do something today that will move you closer to completion.

To follow your heart is to do what you love, your passion! What do you want to have or to be more than anything else? If finances were not an issue and you had all the time in the world and all the resources necessary, what would you do? Remember, whatever the mind can conceive and believe, it can achieve. Your thoughts and your imagination are creating your reality.

The universe gives to those who have faith and trust. Ask what is best for your highest good and will. Whatever you are doing, your energy is being put out in thoughts, words and actions. Is your passion in it? The universe picks up on that energy, passion, power, vigor and intensity, then brings the opportunities to you.

If you get into fear about it not happening, guess what? You create it not happening! Fear blocks. Fear limits. Fear immobilizes. Make a conscious *choice* about what you want in life. Follow your heart! Do what you love; then trust and know all is well. Flow. Allow your inner guidance to show you the best way. Be dedicated and enthusiastic about your life as you follow your heart.

FORGIVE,
RELEASE,
and
ACCEPT
ALL THAT IS.

Do you have resentment against anyone? Do you feel anger, hurt or pain when you think of an individual? If there is anger, wounded pride, ill-will, envy or irritation within you, it will fester. When something festers it contaminates all it touches. Think about that for a moment. You have a precious gift, **Life**, and it has been given to you to do as you wish. What are you doing to enhance yourself and become more loving? Each experience you have is a chance to have a greater awareness of self. Being able to look at the past and see people and situations as gifts makes life richer.

Think of someone who was thoughtless, cruel or harsh to you. Forgive them. Maybe they inflicted pain or suffering, but no matter what happened, it happened. You cannot go back and change the past. You can learn from it, see the gift in it and by doing so, you enhance who you are. Did the situation help you to become stronger, gain willpower, increase determination, acquire a backbone or realize your potential? By *choosing* to let go of the past, acknowledging what happened and giving thanks, your life gets better. Forgive and release. Today, accept all that is as a gift.

> FREEDOM
> is being
> Aware
> of each
> Choice
> you make.

You have the ability to exercise free will. You can spend your time, energy and thoughts worrying about the future or enjoying this moment. It's your *choice.* You can decide to trust Spirit and have faith that all is in Divine order, which then allows you time to 'just be'. Or you can decide to create fears about what is to come.

You can imagine being prosperous and successful or dwell on the lack-of in your life. What are you *choosing* to think? You can invest energy in creating things for the future or focus on past trials, difficulties and regrets. You are free to make *choices* concerning your thoughts, your words and your actions. No one is forcing you; make your own choices.

Are you consciously aware of how tight or loose you hold a pencil when you write or where you last laid your keys? Notice when your emotions are provoked, what are your actions or reactions? What thoughts arise? What do you say and do? Notice if you're coming from a positive or negative space. Just for today, observe your habits, notions, ideas, movements, conduct, speech, chatter, actions, rambling, performance and expressions. Being aware is being free to *choose*.

FREE YOURSELF FROM THE PAST. See the LESSON and GIVE THANKS.

In order to free yourself from the past, first look at what you are thinking that still gives energy to the past. Do you have memories that stir up negative emotions? If so, look at the situation and ask yourself what you learned. What was the lesson? Did you find an inner strength, courage or independence? Do you see a pattern that you want to discontinue? Recognize the gift in it, acknowledge it and give thanks to the Divine.

If you have gratitude about experiences, your vibration changes to a higher level. Do you want to continue reliving past experiences, or open up to new ones? Allow the day to unfold, and be in awareness. Healing takes place through forgiveness.

When your mind goes to a past negative experience, quickly identify the gift in it, see the lesson and give thanks. Then come back to savor the moment at hand. Be willing to free yourself from the past through forgiveness. Forgive everyone. Forgive yourself. Each person is doing the best they can. See the lesson and learn. Today is an experience, tomorrow will be the past. By observing what you do today, you can learn and grow from it.

GIVE THANKS

For Your Progress,

Keep Moving.

Do you appreciate and give recognition to yourself daily? Do you acknowledge your higher power for its part in your life? Life is a gift; what you *choose* to do with this gift is up to you. Every moment is an opportunity to be aware of this wonderful present. The world is evolving. The planet is evolving. You are evolving. Think back to who you were ten years ago. Look at how far you have advanced. Give thanks for that knowledge and understanding. Who were you five years ago? Have you changed? How about two years ago? Give thanks. Keep moving.

You are changing, growing, understanding and becoming more of who you are. You are more than a physical body; you are a spiritual being. You are progressing. Give thanks. You are helping those around you by remembering who you are. As they see you change, they change. We are all one. We help others by helping ourselves. The universe thanks you and the planet's vibrations are raised. The more you open up to the side of you that is nonmaterial, ethereal and mystical, the more you will become pure of heart, moral, humble, reverent and angelic. Give thanks for all you have accomplished. Keep moving.

> **GIVE UNCONDITIONALLY.**
>
> **BE OPEN AND ALLOW YOURSELF TO RECEIVE.**

When you *choose* to give of yourself without any reservations, without any expectations and without any judgments, you will be giving unconditionally. It is when you want something in return or want a response that giving is conditional. Do you want someone to be different before you accept them, thinking that if only they would show more affection, if only they would listen, if only they would be this way or that, then you could love them? That is putting conditions on your giving and not accepting others for who they are.

Giving unconditionally is a higher way of living. Allow yourself to experience emotions both positive and negative. If you want to experience joy, you must be open to experience pain as well; how can we know one without the other? If you close off to one, you close off to the other. Be open. You are free from limitations, free from boundaries and free from restrictions. Respond with appropriate action and words from your heart space. Allow yourself to receive. Be open to others and know you deserve to receive love, light, beauty and joy. By *choosing* to give unconditionally, you open yourself to receive.

**Give up the
need to be
in Control.**

FLOW

What do you get out of being in control? How does it serve you? Are you in balance when in control? Do you know when you are being controlling? Answer these questions now. Allow thoughts and feelings to arise, and give thanks for them. *Choose* not to judge your thoughts; instead just become aware of them. Do you want to give up the need to be in control and turn it over to the Divine? Do you want to be in the flow of life? Remember, Spirit is helping. Things start to happen and opportunities come when you stop challenging everything.

Think of yourself as a magnet pulling in everything you desire to create a wonderful and prosperous life. A magnet does not do anything except be a magnet and all comes to it. You can draw anything to you by being who you are, using all your talents, skills and abilities. Be appreciative, confident and relaxed. Trust and have faith. Turn loose the reins and let the Divine be there for you. Know everything is in Divine order. *Choose* to give up the need to be in control and allow the flow.

**HEALING
IS
YOURS.
RECEIVE.**

What is your belief about healing? Do you believe only medical care can cure or help? Do you believe you can be healed in other ways? Do you believe healing can take place instantaneously? How we heal depends upon our beliefs. Take a look at where you are placing your faith and trust; then you will know who you are and how you will deal with health issues.

We all want a sound body and mind, free of disease and sickness. However, if you do have health problems, how do they serve you? What is the gift? Can you become whole and sound? If something is offered that would benefit you, would you accept? Is it easy or difficult to receive?

No matter what you are faced with today, imagine yourself healthy and feeling privileged to be alive. No matter what you are faced with today, imagine yourself as perfect, whole and full of love. Visualize yourself listening to your body and hearing what is needed for perfect health, such as nourishing foods, approval of self, or releasing negative thoughts and patterns and replacing them with positive ones. Today is a new beginning. Healing is yours. Be open to receive.

**HEAR the
Voice of
the Master.**

LISTEN.

Who do you count on when you hit rock bottom? Do you pray? If so, to whom? Is there a higher power than you in the universe? What does the word 'master' mean to you? Master can mean Lord, God, Divine Guidance, Higher Self, The Universal Mind, A Soul Mind, and many other names. However, if you knew there was a powerful entity out there guiding you to a higher state of consciousness and awareness, would you listen? If you knew that there was a supreme being passing wisdom on to you, would you listen?

What if this higher guidance would lead and inspire you through problems, difficulties and trials, would you listen? If you would believe it and want to hear, become still. Become aware of your breath. Become aware of any thoughts, but do not give them energy. Let them flow through your mind. Visualize a peaceful setting until your body is relaxed and at ease. This is the proper level of awareness for the subconscious mind to receive incoming information. Notice the body is loose and tranquil and the conscious mind passive. Now ask and listen. Listen to your intuition. Then there are times when you **just know**; listen and act upon that.

HOLD A POSITIVE VISION. MIRACLES HAPPEN.

If you have a vision and can believe in it, then you can achieve it. Keep your enthusiasm and energy high. Visualize how you will feel when you accomplish your goal. How will others be affected? Once you make the *choice* to follow your visions and dreams, you can tap into your passion, which is the intense energy of the universe.

With that passion you are able to bring the opportunities and openings to you. You have angels, guides and spirits all helping you to manifest. Extraordinary or unusual events start to happen; you are in the right place at the right time. Miracles happen all the time. You may not have money for the project but an unexpected check arrives in the mail. You have a completed book; you start talking to a stranger whose best friend is a publisher and gets your book published. You are looking for a house and get a sense to take a drive down a street you have never been on, and there is the perfect home. Miracles happen every day. Know it. Believe it. You have the *choice* to hold a positive vision and create a miracle in your life.

Take a moment and imagine what it would be like to be Love and to be Divine. What are the feelings? Are you peaceful or worried? How would you act? Loving or fearful? What would you say? Kind or harsh words? What is your tone of voice? Uplifting or angry? Tap into the Divine Love and the quality of your life will improve.

Our hearts, minds and emotions change and we begin to seek compassion over scorn so others will feel our desire to help. We begin to seek prayer over gossip so others will feel comfort and joy. We begin to seek truth over deceit so others will feel our sincerity. We begin to seek beauty over the banal so others will feel our gentleness. We begin to seek faith over doubt so others will feel our confidence. We begin to seek harmony over separation so others will feel our oneness. We begin to seek gratitude over selfishness so others will feel our appreciation. We begin to seek respect over disrespect so others can feel our consideration.

Choose to believe it, know it and show it. You are Love. You are Divine.

```
I
AM
THAT
I
AM.
```

When you think of who you are, what comes to mind? Reflect upon that before reading on. You are a spiritual being living in a human form. You have many different traits and as you acknowledge all of them you become whole and complete. Think about the following:

I am open minded—I am prejudiced.

I am balanced—I am unstable.

I am strong—I am weak.

I am gentle—I am harsh.

I am happy—I am sad.

I am giving—I am taking.

I am beauty—I am ugly.

I am kind—I am hurtful.

I am persistent—I am lazy.

I am loving—I am hateful.

Choose to watch your behavior. Maybe you are strong 90% of the time but there are moments when you are weak. Therefore, say, "I am strong—I am weak." By acknowledging both and being okay with your weak moments, the acceptance of self is there. No matter what you choose to do in any given moment you are **I am that I am** in that moment.

In Every Moment
You have
Freedom of
CHOICE.
Be
Responsible.

What a great gift the Divine gave us to be able to make our own choices. We can be encouraged and guided by our angels and spirits, but we make the choices. In every moment you have freedom to do or not to do.

Next time you feel you 'have to' or 'need to' do something, say, *"I choose to."* Take this time to think of a particular activity you feel you need to do today: pick up the children, go to work, cook a meal, etc. Say out loud *"I choose to* go to work, *I choose to* cook a meal."* Get in touch with your body when you say it. Now say, **"I need to** cook," and **"I have to** cook." What does that feel like? Strength and power comes from our choices rather than from feeling obligated. We have free will.

Every moment is an opportunity to be free of the past or the future by being present. In the moment of the present, we are free to make the choice that is best for our highest good and will. When we become responsible for our choices we elevate our consciousness, and that is not only serving ourselves and others, but the planet as well. You have the freedom to choose today by being aware of your thoughts, your words and your behavior. Be responsible.

It is not necessary to tell others How to Act, How to Think or How to Be.

Do you believe you are always right? Do you believe you have all the answers? Do you believe you know how others should live? You might be so hard on yourself that you expect others to do as you do. See yourself doing the best you can, with the amount of knowledge and wisdom you have access to at this time; then *choose* to accept yourself. Experience your situations and allow others theirs, without judgment.

Each of us is learning how to find the Divine within and live it. Because each path is different, what works for you might not be what works for others. Ask yourself, "Can a fish live in a tree? Can a monkey live under water?" Each of us has a place where we are most comfortable. Each of us is special and unique and learning how to live in our own environment.

Observe yourself when you are talking with others. What words do you use? Does it sound as though you know what is best for them? Remember, it is not right or wrong—it just is. Don't be so hard on yourself. You can learn when you *choose* to observe. Smile when you catch yourself wanting to tell others how to act, think or be. That is awareness, and in awareness is growth.

Introspection.

Go within and allow the TRUTH to emerge.

QUIET
THE MIND.

This is a time to examine your thoughts and feelings, a time for soul-searching, a time for meditation. Go within and allow the truth to emerge. Sit quietly, observe your breath and become still. Take one thought such as, "Who is God?", or "Why am I here?", or "What is my purpose?" Listen, and repeat the question for several minutes; then listen and trust. If your mind is blank, do it the next day and the next until you feel satisfied with the results. Do you want to know the truth about a situation? Truth about another person? What you need to know is within you. You are an unlimited being.

Quieting the mind is not always easy, but you can do it! In your mind, repeat a question over and over and observe what thoughts arise. Do not give the thoughts energy; just observe and listen. If your mind wanders to another thought, gently bring it back to the current question. Do not get into judgment of what you are hearing; just listen. The truth will emerge, but keep in mind that it may take some time. To journal about your experience can bring insight. This helps the body, mind and spirit work together.

> **JOYFULLY, SOUND WHO YOU ARE.**

You are wonderful no matter what your traits, skills and talents are. Are you a leader with strong willpower, very independent, with a need to be perfect? Are you a mediator who desires to bring peace and harmony to the world and needs to be needed? Do you have creative energy, love to self-express and create beauty from chaos, and have a need to succeed? Are you a hard worker, a planner, very organized, who does not like to be told what to do? Do you like freedom, are willing to take risks, and have a need to know? Are you earthy, very truthful, and have a strong love for family? Are you intelligent, self-reliant, with the energy of a mystic? Do you want justice, want to unify, and need to oppose injustice? Are you a humanitarian, with expanded vision, who wants universal love?

Know you are special and unique. Uniqueness contributes to the world and the world then benefits. Each of us benefits from diversity. As we accept others for who they are, others accept us for who we are. You can be yourself. No more pretending to be someone you're not. No matter who you are and where your traits, strengths and talents lie—be delighted and joyful with who you are.

JUST DO IT!

Be, rather than TRY to Be.

What are you putting off doing until 'later'? Are you postponing a situation because of anxiety or fear of disappointing results? If you notice signs that say do it or have gut feelings to do it, then DO IT! Consider what friends and family are telling you, thank them, and go within to get your answers. Your spirit will be elated and happy. When we are just being, we are allowing, accepting, forgiving and being thankful.

What happens when you *try?* Try and pick up a pen. Try is an attempt—not an end result. If you picked it up then you **did** it. Either you plan to pick up the pen or you really don't want to. Try is an excuse to not complete. Try makes allowances. Try is to just think about it. Try is draining. Try is anguish. Try is considering. Try is a struggle. Try is stress. Say, "I will try and pick up the pen." **Stop** and feel what that's like. Now say, "**I will** pick up the pen." Feel the difference in your body. There is more energy, more willpower when you *choose* to say, "I will..., I am..., I *choose*..." Use the power within to accomplish, create or be anything you desire. Just do it. Enjoy each moment and just be.

When you form an opinion that someone is good or bad, right or wrong, that is judgment and wastes energy. Energy is an expression of how you feel and it affects all those around you. Think of times when you have been around positive people. How does it affect you? What about negative people? Our thoughts are energy, and what you are thinking has a vibration of positive or negative. When you *choose* to judge a person or situation you create that energy. People will know deep within whether you like them or not.

Has someone ever told you, "I love you" and you know it is just words? Is there a predicament you're in or a person that's upsetting you? Stop a moment. What is really happening? Look at their point of view. What would it be like to live as they do, with their parents, children, spouse, background, education, political and spiritual beliefs? As you begin to view them differently, your attitude and mental and emotional fields change. You begin to feel better and more relaxed. Experience the experience. See the lesson and give thanks. Be open and keep judgment out of the experience. Observe all your actions, positive and negative, and gain knowledge from the process.

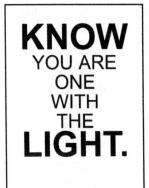

KNOW
YOU ARE
ONE
WITH
THE
LIGHT.

When you truly believe you are Divine, your life and attitude is uplifted. We are grand spiritual beings living in tiny spaces called bodies. Light spreads joy and beauty. Light spreads love to every living thing. Light is free and unlimited. Light is angelic. You are light, and each moment you have a choice to come from the place within where there is light.

The moment you become aware of any fears, doubts, or negative feelings, **stop** and acknowledge them. Once you have recognized them, ask, "Why am I feeling this way and what does this say to me about me?" You have an opportunity to turn them into light. Look at the whole situation; see what the root of it is. Are these feelings a pattern you react to? What is the lesson or gift in this situation?

Now ask yourself, "Do I want to stay in this space?" If not, then you have the *choice* to turn fears, doubts or negative feelings over into love and light through visualization. Think of yourself as weightless and cheerful. Imagine you are light—laughing, smiling and being happy. Become light-hearted and care-free. You elevate yourself in consciousness when you make conscious choices instead of reacting out of habit. Know you are one with the light. You are divine love.

LAUGH LAUGH

Doesn't it feel wonderful to express yourself with laughter? It has been said that laughter is food for the soul. When you allow yourself to find humor in situations, that releases strain, tension and pressure on the body. Laughter reduces stress. Stress is unhealthy. Laughter reduces worry. Worry is wasted energy. Energy is valuable to your health.

Is this message a confirmation that you are laughing? If so, continue laughing because many people are benefiting from your humor. When you are under mental or emotional pressure find something funny: a movie, a book, or friends that create laughter. Can you find something ridiculous in your life right now? Why must everything be so somber? Create a lighter side! Children are funny. Life is funny. Animals are funny. Nature is funny. Adults are funny. *Choose* to see life differently. Recall a situation or event when you laughed so hard your side ached. Smile and know you are doing the best you can under your circumstances— and so is everyone else. Demonstrate your happiness through the sounds of laughter.

Let Go of 'Should I'. 'Could I' and 'What If'.

Think of a time when you said "Should I?, or "Could I?," or "What if?" How much time and energy was wasted in indecision? If you are sensing something and can't explain why, it is a 'just know' feeling. Your family, friends or society may be saying no. Go ahead and just do it. Remember, "Could I?" is lack of confidence. Say, "Yes, Yes, Yes" to yourself. You can do it! Think, "Yes, Yes, Yes, I can create it!"

You have all the guidance within you to accomplish, create, maneuver, achieve, perform, fulfill and succeed. When you make a decision from within, all your vitality and passion comes forth to make it happen. "What if?" keeps you stagnant. "What if?" drains your energy. "What if" gives you doubts.

Stop. Face your fears, your challenges, your suspicions and your beliefs. Imagine the worst-case scenario. What would you do? Know you can handle anything by taking the responsibility for your actions through your beliefs, your emotions and your thoughts. You are powerful within. Know it. Let go of 'should I,' 'could I', and 'what if'. **Choose** to be unlimited.

**Limitless
Bliss
is yours.**

ILLUMINATE!

By limiting yourself you create a boundary that does not exist, and therefore you choose not to go beyond. You *can* go beyond, but often because of past experiences, patterns or belief systems, you limit yourself.

Take a moment and imagine you have unlimited strength, courage, confidence and abundance. What would this feel like? In order to be confident, you must feel confident. In order for you to be abundant, you must feel abundant and want abundance for others as well. Would that bring you bliss? Bliss is extreme happiness and joy. Imagine yourself in a state of beauty and bliss. Where are you and what are you doing?

Do you want to be unlimited? Then say that you want to be unlimited. The desire first, the action next. Act as if you already have that talent, skill, money or meaningful relationship. To illuminate is to light up. Light up the world! Light up those around you. The world wants your light to shine. Know you are light. When you are full of bliss inside, you illuminate on the outside.

**LOVE
and
UNDERSTAND
YOURSELF.
HONOR
YOU.**

To love and understand yourself is to stay out of judgment and not compare your actions with others'. You are one of a kind. Do you believe that? Are you not unique? Are not all snowflakes, leaves and sea shells different? They look similar but they are not the same, just as no two humans are the same. No one can take your place. You have your own special energy, your own set of fingerprints and your own way of thinking and being.

To love ourselves is not always easy. Sometimes we're critical of our own actions and words when it is not necessary. We get into judgment about ourselves. Next time you find yourself being critical, stop and replace it with love. Honor *you*. Know you are giving to the world in your own way and that others can benefit. Recognize your special gifts.

Remember, you have done the best you can under the circumstances with the amount of knowledge and wisdom you have access to at this time. As you begin to honor yourself, you also honor all others. Smile and give thanks for their presence in your life. Give yourself recognition for your achievements and talents. Love and understand where you are coming from, and honor who you are.

MAKE CHOICES THAT FEEL GOOD.

Every day of your life you are faced with thousands of *choices*: what to cook, what to eat, what to wear, what to do, to go or not to go, to call this person or not, to go to work or stay home. Every hour you make hundreds of *choices*, but many people act from habit rather than being aware of their choices.

Have you ever driven a car somewhere and then not remembered how you got to your destination? Or put your keys down and forgot where they were? What were you thinking in that moment of laying your keys down? To be aware of life, you must be awake and conscious of your thoughts. Thoughts can monopolize your day and you will be swept away into the past by them. Thoughts can throw you into the future and you'll miss the smile of a loved one.

Daily life can be repetitious; however, growth comes when you're aware of your *choices*: the drive home, writing, taking a shower, doing dishes, or talking with friends. When someone asks you to go to the movies and you don't want to, politely say 'no'. A friend wants to borrow your car and you can't explain it but it doesn't feel right, then politely say 'no'. Be responsible for your choices. Go with that "I just know" feeling. Within you are the answers, so make choices that feel good!

Manifest.

UNLIMITED
THOUGHTS
Are Yours.

CREATE.

What do you want to manifest? What is it you are not creating? What is inside you saying, "Do it;" or "Go for it;" or "Create it?" Now is the time to manifest. Unlimited thoughts are yours. Is it a belief system that says, "I can't; I'm not good enough; that's silly; I don't have the finances; it takes too long; I'm not smart enough; or I'm too old?" Once you get in touch with the limiting belief, *choose* to change your thinking about it.

Each day think thoughts that support your idea, your project or your dream. Become aware of limiting self-talk such as: "I'll do it later; I don't have the time; I don't have the energy; it wouldn't be perfect; no one will like it," and on and on. Replace those old thoughts with new ones. Tell yourself, "I am energetic, I am intelligent, I am independent, I am strong." Imagine yourself being that way. What does it feel like? How do you act?

Face any fears associated with your idea, project or dream: fear of rejection, failure, hurt or disappointment. Imagine success and abundance. Imagine yourself unlimited; what's that like? Imagine others loving the idea, supporting you, complimenting you; then bring your power back and create what you desire. Know you and your thoughts are unlimited. Believe it. Manifest it.

**MANIFEST
Your Dreams.**

ALIGNMENT
is called for
at this time.

What are your dreams? What are your aspirations? What do you imagine yourself doing? What do you love to do? Anything you love to do brings joy. Joy is love. Love your work. Work does not have to be a negative experience; it can be fun and enjoyable. Enjoy what you do.

In order to fulfill your dreams you must first know what they are. If you are not sure yet, take time and think of what you love, what brings pleasure and satisfaction. How can you create that in your life? What are you doing now that you do not like to do, but feel obligated to continue doing? Find different ways to view the situation and bring positive feeling and fun into it. Adjust yourself in a way that you feel balanced.

Create what you love; think of jobs that will support your strengths, talents and abilities. You are capable of manifesting your dreams by *choosing* to take appropriate action and aligning yourself with what you desire. Go for it. Stay out of fear. Know and believe the universe is here to support and guide you. Align with higher guidance and listen to your heart; then manifest your dreams.

MOTIVATE
-SELF-

Use Your
Creativity.

What can you do to create your desire? What is it you long to do? What do you wish for? Yearn for? Aspire to? Be still and think of what brings you joy. Once you are in touch with what you want, that energy creates the motivation. The energy will be in your thoughts, your words and your actions. The motivation will be there, and the willpower to create it. The attitude behind the activity affects the end results.

You can achieve anything you desire through motivating self and using creativity. We often become tired or sluggish because energy is drained through thoughts of worry or indecision. You have the opportunity to motivate through positive self-talk, calming your emotions and nurturing your body.

Creativity can be used from moment to moment rather than on a large scale. Think of moments when you are standing in a long line of negative people waiting to be served; what could you do to uplift or bring humor to that situation? That's creativity. Monitor yourself from one activity to another and see if you feel motivated. If not, creatively change the situation.

The unfamiliar to you can be scary. However, if you take the action to explore, then rewards and satisfaction can be gained. There is power and growth in taking risks. There is strength in stretching beyond your limits.

To go beyond that fear into a place of faith and trust is when your life gets better—better because you decided to have hope and aspire to something greater. By putting your confidence in your guidance and Higher Self, miracles happen.

Traveling into the unfamiliar is really discovering your strength and what you are capable of being. As you investigate your self physically, mentally, emotionally and spiritually you open up to new experiences, new possibilities and unlimited thinking. By recognizing more of your spiritual self, your skills and abilities are enhanced.

Now is the time to move into a place you are not familiar with and see what it brings. The unknown does not have to be scary; believe and feel assured you are safe. Move into the unknown and Just Be. ***Choose*** to have confidence and go for it.

MOVE with the Currents of CHANGE.

When situations begin to change, what do you do? Fight or contest it? Is there resistance? Do you stand up to it, balk, or just get frustrated and confused? Imagine a current of water. What happens when the water hits the rocks? What does the water do when it confronts an obstacle: it flows and moves smoothly around.

Now visualize yourself balanced, stable, and listening to your own inner guidance. How does it feel? Have faith and trust that all is in divine order. Know you can flow and move smoothly with the currents of change. You are on your course, just as the water is on its course. Be in the flow. Do not allow the barriers, stumbling blocks or snags to stop your forward motion. When guided by Spirit, any change is for betterment of self.

You have a choice to be poised and peaceful about change, through observation of what's happening. See the advantages and benefits. Enjoy the moment. Know that each season is precious. Each season brings its own joy. Each season brings its own beauty. Each season brings its own blessings. Allow your life to move with the currents of change.

'OBSERVE'

OPPORTUNITIES
ARE COMING
YOUR WAY.

Opportunities may not always be presented as you expect; they come in a variety of ways. It is important to stay open and observe. They may not come as quickly as you desire, so be patient. Focus on the essence of what you desire, allow it to unfold, and enjoy the results.

If you want a career that brings satisfaction, then get in touch with the feeling of being satisfied and allow the universe to bring the opportunity. You must know what you want in order for it to come to you, and then believe it will come. Ask your angels and guides to be with you when considering what road to take. Trust the voice within. Listen to yourself rather than to what others are saying. Allow your guidance to show the way. The knowing is within you.

When the opportunity comes, do not worry about the fine details. Do not worry about the outcome. Just go for it. Trust that all will fall into place. Life presents the opportunities; you must take the action. Observe, because timing is the key. All details must be in order. Opportunities come when the situation and people are ready. Watch attentively in your circumstances. You can create what you desire. Opportunities are coming.

Observe Your Habits.

Are they Nourishment to Your Body?

How do you treat your body? What are your exercise habits? What are your eating patterns? What do you "feed" your mind? When you begin to analyze your routine you can begin to question yourself. What can you do today for betterment of your body, mind and spirit?

When you are out of balance, the body may feel stress or tension. The mind can be confused and awareness is shut down. Examine how stressed or relaxed your body feels from one activity to another. If stressed, take a deep breath and relax. Are your thoughts positive or negative? If they are negative, change your thinking or attitude.

Make the decision to observe your habits, your choice of words, the inflection of your voice, and your actions and reactions. You are on your way to enlightenment. Physically, you are what you are in this moment. Emotionally, you are what you are in this moment. Mentally, you are what you are in this moment. Spiritually, you are what you are in this moment. Today, observe your thoughts, words and actions and see if they are nourishing, positive, healthy and inspiring.

OBSERVE YOURSELF and You Will Know Who You Are.

The key to enlightenment is to *"know thyself."* You may ask, "How do I do that?" Pay attention to your habits, thoughts, speech, feelings and performance. Observe what you do in situations, how you respond to people, and your tone of voice. The more you know who you are, the more enlightened you become.

As you become aware of any patterns or habits, celebrate that. Being aware is a step in a new direction! To become aware of a habit is like finding a treasure. The treasure is you. Remember who you are. Stay out of judgment of self and others and know we are all on our own path to enlightenment. Know we are all connected, we are one. Allow compassion to dwell within you.

When you view yourself from a higher perspective, you can rise above the situation and consider all viewpoints. What do you think and feel? What do others think and feel? Allow yourself to see life through someone else's eyes. You are also expanding who you are when you allow others to be a reflection for you. You cannot recognize something in another that is not within you. Through observation you will know who you are and who you are not.

OPEN THE DOOR *LISTEN* TO KNOWLEDGE.

You have a storehouse of information within you, with facts and figures to draw upon. When you are listening to guidance, the right action and words will come effortlessly. Every experience is an opportunity to gain knowledge and use your wisdom. Every person is unique and has a special connection with higher guidance.

Listen to your guidance by quieting the mind, opening up to your intuition and acting upon that which you know. When you begin to allow new possibilities, new ways of thinking and new ways of being, then wonderful events happen in your life. Know that within you is the knowledge; open the door and listen. Ask yourself, "What happens when fear arises? Do I listen or do I shut down? Do I run away? Do I pretend it's not there? Do I pray? Do I turn within and listen to find answers? Do I ask my guidance for assistance?"

Each situation is different, but through observation of self you can start to see patterns and blocks created by fear. In that moment of awareness, you can *choose* to do something different. The knowledge and wisdom are there; listen and know you have all the answers. Remember who you are. You are more than this physical body. Open up and listen to your spiritual self.

OPEN TO A MORE EXPANSIVE VIEW.

Your spirituality is expanding. Allow yourself to understand different points of view and accept others for who they are. Maybe it is a time for more mindfulness in day-to-day living. Maybe it is time to become whole and peaceful.

Take a moment and review your present situation. Are you only seeing your point of view? Are you being biased? Are you being narrow-minded? Are you making judgments? Just for today, see life differently. Pretend you are an eagle flying high overhead, seeing all perspectives. You can view everything that is happening. Do you see how you fit in? What is your role? Do you like what is happening? If not, you have the freedom to change. When you change, others change.

Is there love and compassion, or fear and anxiety? We are all connected, we are all one. By understanding your views about life, your awareness of self increases, helping you to make decisions that are best for all concerned. You can come from a greater awareness. Be the eagle; observe and understand from a higher perspective. Be open to a more expansive view.

OPEN up to Miracles and Receive.

Miracles happen every day. Do you believe in miracles? A miracle is an extraordinary or unusual event that is considered to be a manifestation of the Divine or supernatural power. Visualize yourself doing what you love, using your gifts and talents in a positive way. Positive change produces positive results. Your thinking, your posture, your attitude, your actions and words all play an important part in creating your future.

As you change and accept the Divine within you, you move into a new way of thinking and being, and miracles happen. Is there enough financial abundance in your life? Look at how you think and feel about money. Are you happy for other people's success and prosperity? Rejoice for other people's wealth instead of being jealous or resentful.

Keep your heart open to receive! How do you express your feelings about money? Do you shop at expensive department stores or thrift marts? What is your intention shopping there? How does it make you feel? Do you deserve the best or settle for less? Do you hate paying your bills? If so, change your approach and pay them with love! Open the channel to receive more. Are you ready to receive gifts from Spirit? Know it, believe it, and allow miracles to come.

OPEN UP YOUR POWERS OF OBSERVATION AND LEARN.

How do you open up your powers of observation? Practice being present and observant by doing three things. First, ground yourself by sensing your feet. Is the weight of your body on them heavy or light?

Second, open your vision by remaining focused on an object in front of you, then with your peripheral vision look to the far left above and below and to the far right above and below. Do not take your eyes off the original object. Now you have full vision. Be in touch with how that feels.

Third, imagine you have an angel on your shoulder, and that angel is your observer. The observer will watch your habits, the tone of your voice, your speech, actions, reactions, emotions, thoughts, the way you walk, the words you choose, how tight you hold the steering wheel, your facial expressions, everything. The observer is just observing, not judging.

The key to enlightenment is to know thyself. You can open up your powers of observation and learn. Learn who you are, because who you are is Divine. Life will occur without force, strain or pressure. The power of *choice* is yours. Ground yourself, open your vision, observe and learn.

OPEN
YOUR
HEART
SPACE.

Ask yourself, "Am I sincere? Am I straight-forward and honest? Am I objective and responsive? Am I a giver or a taker?" As you become aware of your thoughts, words, tone of voice and actions, the more you begin to know who you are.

Are there some people you choose to love and others you hold at a distance? The ones you hold at a distance may be the ones most healed by your love. You have drawn this message as a reminder not to be critical and to open your heart space and have compassion for self. It is not always easy to open your heart and love when you have been hurt so many times, yet that is the way to higher living. To open your heart is to love without conditions.

Each day presents you with opportunities to help others by being in your heart space. Begin to notice your thoughts, choice of words, tone of voice and deeds. Are they heart-felt? Give thanks for any insight. Today, *choose* to open your heart space and be more compassionate with yourself and all those who cross your path.

OPPORTUNITIES
for Growth
are Coming
Your way.

ALLOW.

Changes and opportunities are coming, and with change comes growth. Growth can be a challenge. Remember, you have your angels, guides and spirits with you always. Can you feel their presence now? Acknowledge them. Change allows you to experience more of who you are, and is an opportunity in itself. It may be about career, a special relationship or financial freedom. To allow change is also to have patience. Patience may not come easily, yet we grow from learning how to be patient.

Remember a time when you were in the right place at the right time. That was an opportunity which you allowed. Think of the time and energy saved by not pushing or tugging. This is a time to listen to the voice within and allow the opportunities to unfold.

Trust yourself when you see the opportunity. If it is a risk, call upon your inner strength and courage. Then use your skills and abilities to go for it and come out a winner. Remember, opportunities might not come the way you think, so be open-minded and make decisions that are best for you. Allow the opportunities to unfold.

PACE Yourself. Stamina will INCREASE. ALLOW Quiet Time.

At what rate of speed are you moving through life? Are you under a lot of stress? Are you relaxed? Where are you putting your priorities: job, family, health or social life? Pause between activities and check your body for stamina. When you decide not to rush from one performance to the next, your physical, mental and spiritual self will benefit.

Take a breather and become aware of any tension, confusion or feelings at that moment. Know you have the endurance for all things. Know Spirit is with you. By taking mini-breaks throughout the day, you'll feel better and your actions and words will be clearer. Do you feel you do not have enough time? You will create more time when you have a clear head because mistakes are fewer, there is less chance of stress and fatigue, and you spend less time looking for lost items and redoing things.

Make the decisions that are best for your health, mental clarity and inner peace. Allow quiet time. Why would you choose not to do so? If you want more stamina, then *choose* to pace yourself. Take mini-breaks, slow down, breathe and allow quiet time.

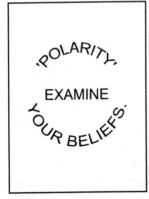

POLARITY

EXAMINE

YOUR BELIEFS

When you begin to examine your convictions and question why you act, behave and reason as you do, you are desiring to raise your consciousness. When you begin to challenge your views on morals, faith, and doctrines you begin to understand more about why you do what you do. Understanding brings about compassion for self, and compassion for self can improve the quality of your life.

Start trusting in your inner guidance rather than what others think. You might be discarding old patterns, old beliefs and old ways of thinking, but you can become stronger, more vibrant, and full of joy. When you are doing something because someone tells you it is best and you *know* that it isn't, you dampen your own spirit.

You were taught what is right by others. Now is the time to go within and know what is best for you. Take charge of your life. What is polarity to you? Do you know who you are? Examine your beliefs by researching, exploring, studying and observing. Remember, through observation of self you will know thyself and that is the key to enlightenment.

PRAY AND BELIEVE.

All things are possible when you communicate with a higher power. When you express your hopes, dreams and desires to the universe, you must believe that they are heard. When you make an earnest request for Divine guidance, know the answers will come, though perhaps not the way you expect. This is often why people feel their prayers are not answered: they expect it to be a certain way and wonder why their pleas are ignored.

The Divine is always with you, always supporting you, always encouraging you—and if you *choose* to believe it, you will feel it and know it and receive it. Your attitude, behavior, words and actions will change for the better. Trust and believe you are being heard. Then listen. Put your faith in Higher Self rather than in your surroundings, society, family or friends. Listen to other people's viewpoints, but trust your own guidance.

To know is to believe. To believe is to accept. To accept is to receive. To receive is to know. You come full circle in your thinking and your being. You are more than this physical body. You are a spiritual being working with a higher power. Pray and believe.

PURIFICATION is Helpful at this time.

What would it feel like to be free of blame, self-condemnation or negativity? How would you feel if there were no past experiences haunting you? Next time you bathe, imagine the water as sacred, holy and healing. Imagine that as it goes over your head and body, you are being cleansed of all pessimism and charged with vitality, beauty and clarity. The water purifies your aura. The water takes away all the stress, confusion, pain and uncertainty.

You are moral and full of integrity. You are genuine and flawless. You have a pure heart. Do you want to remove toxins from your body? What might you do today to internally cleanse? What foods or beverages might your body require right now? Purge your body of those foods that are not healthy for you. Bless your food before eating.

Are your thoughts clear at this time? Wash away thinking that is not honest, sincere, or worthy. Wipe away past experiences that are not uplifting and decide to turn them over to a higher power. Freshen up those thoughts and feel the lightness it brings. Devote today to purifying your world inside and out.

**RELEASE
Attachment
on all Levels.**

**Mentally
Emotionally
Physically**

What do you feel attached to? What do you feel belongs to you? As you ponder these questions, become aware of what you are feeling and experiencing. Are you attached to a home and don't want to lose it? Are you attached to a job and don't want to find another? Are you attached to a person and feel that if you lose them, you will have nothing? When you become aware of something being taken away and you fight to keep it, you're going against the flow of life. Life changes. You change.

Release attachments mentally, emotionally and physically. Release what no longer works. Become aware of your beliefs, your fears, your emotions and your thoughts. A belief can be faced, released and changed. Fears can be faced, released and changed. Emotions can be faced, released and changed. Thoughts can be faced, released and changed.

You are in full power of your life. You can be in the flow. How do you want to experience your experience? In love or fear? Challenge your beliefs, emotions and thoughts. Release attachments. You have a choice.

Take a look at what control means to you. Is control wanting others to do what you want? Is control wanting everything your way? Is control the power to direct situations? Is control just an influence over others? What would happen if you were not in control? Free yourself from controlling and dominating others and being so hard on yourself. Your body will appreciate it. Your body will become more relaxed.

When you stop exercising your authority over every detail and allow, your life gets better. Strong control takes a lot of energy. If you believe in a higher power, then turn over your problems and difficulties to it and allow the flow of life. Flowing is a continuous movement. Flowing is not pushing or pulling but freely allowing Spirit to bring opportunities and advancements to you.

Imagine yourself flowing from one activity to another, knowing a force much greater than you is guiding and directing. Enjoy being with your family and friends. Can you enjoy what you do from moment to moment? If not, why not? Think about it. Release control and allow the flow. Enjoy the moment.

**Release
Judgements.**
ALLOW
LOVE
from your
Heart
Space.

What is judgment? Judgment is an opinion about someone or something being moral, immoral, dishonest, good, ugly, smart, etc. Begin to take full responsibility for your thoughts and judgments. If you feel you are being judged, blamed or victimized, stop! In that moment send love to that person because they may be coming from fear, lack of self-love, low self-esteem, hurt or pain. When you can come from love rather than buying into other people's judgments, that increases your own inner power.

Release judgments about yourself and others. Allow love from your heart. You can choose to love rather than judge. Others are experiencing and learning, too. Open your heart space, forgive and release judgments. Observe your thoughts and the next time your mind is in judgment **stop**, understand the other point of view and open your heart. Listen and explore why they feel, think or act the way they do. Allow them to be them and you to be you. Release the judgment and love them for who they are. Each of us does things differently. If they could do better, they would. Love unconditionally. Release judgment about self and others.

> **Remember Laughter and Humor are Powerful Healers.**

Can you find humor in life's situations? If not, why? Life can be very funny when you allow yourself to see the comical side. Laughter is medicine for the body. It heals. Find humor throughout the day; it is there. Once you start to laugh, others do as well. Laughter is contagious. Think of all the people who benefit when you allow yourself to experience fun. Others around you will follow your lead and enjoy. Laughter uplifts. Laughter heals.

Take a moment to look at a situation that doesn't seem very funny to you. Is there a cosmic joke? Did you ask for this, but didn't expect this result? This might be an opportunity to rise above the situation and see how you created it. Find the humor.

Maybe this message is a reminder for you to continue on your path laughing, enjoying and creating a wonderful space for yourself and others. Each day you make thousands of *choices* through your thoughts, spoken words and attitude. How many of them are bringing you laughter? Laughter and humor are powerful healers. You have the capacity, skills, potential, intelligence and strength to create something miserable or create something humorous. It's your **choice.**

REMEMBER
YOU ARE
SPECIAL.
HONOR THAT.

You are unique. You are exceptional. You are not like anyone else. Give yourself credit. Respect who you are. As you read this, what feelings or emotions arise? Are you saying 'yes, yes, yes', or discounting yourself? What would it feel like to be held in high respect? What posture do you have? What words and tone of voice do you use? If you were toasted for your talents and abilities, would you bask in it?

Every day you make choices as to how you feel about yourself through your thoughts, words, emotions and actions. You have the power within to stop any critical voices about not being good enough, or smart enough, or pretty enough, etc. The moment you become aware of a discounting voice, **stop**—and decide to feel successful, intelligent, beautiful. Then say something positive about yourself.

Remember, you are special. Honor that. Can you feel special? Why are you special? Is not each person special in the eyes of the Divine? There is only one you. Be thankful! Take charge of your thoughts, your actions and your words about who you are. You are love and beauty. See how special you are, and honor that.

**Remember
You are
the Teacher
as well as
the Student.**

In life you have many opportunities to inspire friends, family, children and even strangers. A true teacher doesn't tell others how to act or what to say or do unless they are asked, but rather teaches by example. You can assist others by being an example for them to learn from.

Each person or situation that comes across your path is an opportunity for you to learn and grow from. Someone may appear that could be a mentor for you or you for them and by not speaking, sharing or being who you are, you might miss a wonderful opportunity. Each of us is here to be inspired and to inspire others. Each of of has the perfect moment to give or receive, listen or speak, to be positive or negative. In that moment of being aware, your choice of what to do or not to do plays an important part in the next moment.

Remember, others learn from you: your attitude, your strength, your words, your beauty and your behavior, and you learn from them. You are the teacher and the student. Pay attention to what you are doing or saying and that will bring you into the moment. By being in the moment you can choose to learn, laugh, smile, enjoy—and inspire others to do the same.

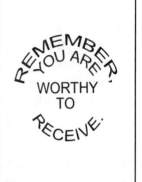

In your childhood were you told that you were not valuable or good enough? If you do not feel deserving, acceptable, reliable, decent, good, moral or trustworthy, then it is difficult to receive. Overcome this by seeing yourself in a different light. Know that you are worthy to receive.

Remember, every person in your life has helped to mold you into who you are today. Each person taught you to have a greater understanding of yourself. They played a part just as people act out a play, with each character having their own significance. You are now a new person, and in a different season of your life playing a different role.

Do you want to receive? Then feel it! Do you receive compliments, healing, money and success graciously? If not, why not? You are worthy to have what you desire because you are deserving and remarkable in the universe's eyes. Do you want a wonderful and loving relationship? See yourself as wonderful, loving and worthy. Whatever you desire is yours and can be manifested through your thoughts, words and deeds. Be open and receive from the universe. You can have a greater life-style filled with joy by remembering you are worthy to receive.

Do you have feelings of agitation or anxiety? Do you have expectations or presumptions? Are you afraid or worried about a situation? Whatever is going on, **STOP**. Get in touch with your breath and be thankful for something. Remove the fear.

Take a moment and imagine your guardian angel, spirit guide or higher power watching over you, guiding you with every step you take, holding your hand, helping you, and wanting you to trust. *Choose* to take the step of faith and release the negativity into their hands. Imagine that you are safe and secure; how does it feel? Let your body relax into that sensation.

When you are in fear, fear brings negativity, negativity brings depression and soon you are faced with feelings of being overwhelmed or submerged in a sea of problems. This is a vicious cycle. Negativity brings more negativity. However, you have the *choice* to stop it. Take action to correct the situation. If you have done what you can and it's out of your hands, then no longer give it energy. Trust and have faith. Allow. Know you are okay. See the humor and the Divine in all things. Removing the fear allows life to unfold.

Seek Solutions rather than Focusing on Problems.

What are the problems, difficulties or uncertainties you have today? Instead of thinking about the problem, what can you do to take care of it? Think of different solutions and put your energy into the solution rather than the difficulty. Being worried sends negative energy out into the universe. Remember, what you put out comes back to you. How do you want to use your energy, for betterment or destruction?

This moment is all you have and you can choose to uplift or invalidate. Keep in mind that you can focus on what you want rather than what you don't want in this moment. There are always *choices* and one of them is to turn it all over to a higher power and allow the flow. Ask for guidance from the Divine. Know a solution will come and let it be.

If you believe in miracles, then a solution can come at any given moment. Solutions can come in a variety of ways: through nature, the written or spoken word, a thought, a soft voice, a stranger or even your pet. There is no set way for you to receive. Stop focusing on problems and be open to hear, be open to see, and be open to solutions.

> **See the different Viewpoints. Validate them and make the Choice best for YOU.**

Each of us is unique and has a place on the wheel of life. Each path is a spoke on the wheel which leads to the center and the center is Divine. By taking the time to understand others' viewpoints, your own life can be enriched. When you *choose* to listen with an open mind about what others think and how they feel, you will have expansion within yourself. To listen to and not judge other people's beliefs and viewpoints helps you to become whole. Remember, you are part of the whole, and they are part of the whole.

Through understanding and love, the world can become a better place. If others feel they know what is best for you, listen and thank them. Then go within and listen to inner guidance. When you do what others want you to do rather than what you want, you are not validating yourself.

Listen to what others think is best and do not blame or criticize them, but make the choice that is best for you. It is so important to be in touch with your intuition, that inner knowingness. Taking responsibility for your *choices* gives you power to create, to manifest, to have confidence and love. Validate yourself and others. Then do what is best for you!

> **See the gifts Provided by others. They are a MIRROR to you!**

All of us came from the same source, The Divine. The Divine created us as unique individuals with traits and emotions, such as: love-hate, happy-sad, honest-dishonest, strong-weak, peaceful-warlike, enthusiastic-lazy, sharp-dull, kind-rude, giver-taker, etc. What you can recognize in others are also parts of who you are. You are all of these traits, behaviors and more.

Take a moment and think about this: every person you have ever known has given you a gift. Isn't that wonderful? The gift is who you are. You can be strong or weak at any given moment. Maybe you're strong 85% of the time and will not allow yourself to be weak. Therefore, when you see weakness in another, that is a reflection of the weakness you have not accepted in yourself, and it annoys you. It could also be you are weak 85% of the time, so weak people reflect back what you dislike in yourself.

You cannot recognize what you do not have within. We all have our own beauty and beast. You have opportunities to see the gifts provided by others and accept them as part of the whole. We are all one.

See what Expectations are causing YOU to Experience!!!

Life has a wonderful way of unfolding, if we allow it. However, if you expect life to be one way or another and it doesn't happen, you have actually set yourself up for disappointment and frustration, and then think it is someone else's fault. Ask yourself, is there really fault or blame? When you take full responsibility for your thoughts and actions, you will feel better about your decisions and know you are coming from a place of power.

Think of what you want from your career, your relationships or a situation and allow it to unfold, rather than expecting it to be only one way. Listen to your intuition; allow it to guide you. Become aware of the expectations you create. When you realize you've formed an opinion, examine it, then think again.

To look forward to something gives us hope. Many times when we are expecting something to happen and it doesn't, we get out of balance and it turns into worry. Valuable energy is lost, energy that can be used more wisely. In that moment of worry, go within and ask your guidance for assistance. Allow the situation to unfold. Stay in balance. Become aware of your experience.

What are you capable of becoming? Are your abilities and talents being used and developed? What could you do to improve? Is this a time to increase, develop and strengthen your awareness of self? Your gifts, talents, skills and abilities are waiting to be used to elevate you to higher consciousness.

Become aware of your habits, your thoughts and your existence. What habits do you have that hold you back or help you to become all you can be? Are your thoughts helping you to reach your potential? Do you criticize or uplift and encourage yourself? Words are powerful. What are you telling yourself to reach your potential? If you desire something better, now is the time to expand. Go for it.

Imagine someone giving you a treasure chest and when you open it, you find it is filled with all your potential: courage, faith, trust, truth, independence, creativity, knowledge and so much more. It is all yours to use any time. Call upon the Divine to assist you when you are ready. The Divine is always with you and wants you to succeed, to heal, to have healthy relationships, and to be abundant. See your potential. You have the abilities to expand and become whatever you desire.

See Your Present Situation as a Gift. **GIVE THANKS!**

Take a moment to review what is going on in your life right now. Are you happy or sad? Are you excited or depressed? Are you moving forward or feeling stuck? Are you free to do as you will or feeling bound by obligations?

Today you have an opportunity to find a gift in this situation. Wherever you are is perfect for you at this moment. Your inner power is increased once you recognize your present situation as a gift. What are you harvesting from it: patience, firmness, strength, equilibrium, self-control, courage, stamina, persistence, gratitude or boldness? What is going on for you right now is a chance to learn and find the gift. Remember, each experience is an opportunity to have a greater understanding of self, which empowers you for the next experience.

Become aware of all the emotions and feelings that arise. Honor them. Is your present situation helping you to be creative or stagnated, abundant or lacking, positive or negative, compassionate or unkind? If you are learning, you are growing—and that is a gift in itself. Today, view your present situation as positive. Give thanks.

SIMPLIFY.
Be Yourself.
SMILE.

What would it take to simplify your life? Would you benefit by decreasing responsibility? Would it mean getting rid of material things and if so, what? Would saying 'no' to others who want your help simplify your life? Is being detached to outcomes the answer?

Only you know what is best for you, and only you can make that *choice*. By being who you are without concern for what others think, and following your own inner guidance, your truth will emerge. Do you approve of yourself? If not, why not? Start affirming all the things you like about you. If you like who you are, others will as well. You do not have to put on a facade. Express gratitude for who you are. What do you love about being you?

Think of all the ways you can simplify. Make it fun and pleasurable for yourself. The more you view things as fun and enjoyable, the more you receive out of life. Life is what you decide to make it; it can be fun or miserable. Today be yourself. Stay detached from what others might be thinking or doing and smile at everyone you meet. Others will be delighted. Make the world a better place by being you. Smile.

SPEAK YOUR TRUTH.

Express Your Viewpoint.

Sometimes you may hold back your truth because you feel it won't be accepted, will be discounted, or that you might hurt someone's feelings. ***Choosing*** to express what you believe in, your truth, actually gives you power. All viewpoints are valid. The more you decide to express yourself in a loving and kind way, the more confident you become in who you are.

Ask yourself, "What is my truth? What do I believe? Is what I think coming from my parents' beliefs? Or what my friends have told me or from the books I've read? Or is it what my religion has taught me?" Become silent and allow your truth to be heard. Every day you have an opportunity to express what you think, what you feel and what you believe. Observe yourself in conversations and become aware of your thoughts and feelings.

Notice when you ***choose*** to be quiet and when you ***choose*** to express yourself. The more you pay attention to yourself in situations, the more you learn about who you are, and in that awareness of self you have the opportunity to grow in confidence and spirituality. Remember, you benefit as well as others when you express your viewpoint and speak your truth.

What happens when you feel an impulse to go somewhere, call someone, write a letter or take a different route? Do you follow through on that impulse? What has been your experience when you have done so? We all have incidents where we have acted upon intuition and often they prove to be very valuable. When you become aware of those tendencies or stimuli and honor them, your life can be more rewarding and exciting.

Become aware of any ideas that are self-generated (without apparent external cause) and follow through on them; the results may be beneficial for your growth. Remember, Spirit worked through you to pick up this book, now you have a confirmation with the words: yes, yes, yes. Do it! Say 'yes' to life, say 'yes' to what you aspire to, say 'yes' to change, say 'yes' to release, say 'yes' to healing, say 'yes' to awareness, say 'yes' to listening and say 'yes' to love.

Your inner guidance, strength and power are available to you at all times. Say 'yes' to yourself today and just be. Whenever you get that feeling of inner knowingness, say 'yes' and do it. When guided, say 'yes' to spontaneity.

SPREAD YOUR WINGS. *FEEL LOVE.*

Do you believe in angels? Do you believe angels can be humans, animals, invisible or anything? Could you be an angel? Imagine you are an angel. What feelings and emotions would you have? What facial expressions, body postures and gestures? Angels have wings; how does that feel and how large or small are they? Experience yourself flying. What would your day be like?

Now feel the **Divine Love**, the highest form of love. Love without conditions. Love without judgment. Love without expectations. Love with respect and admiration. Love with affection and passion. Love with kindness and thoughtfulness. Love with reverence and empathy. This love is in harmony with all those it comes in contact with.

Continue to imagine this Divine love coming through the top of your head, filling every cell, every muscle, every fiber in your body and overflowing so it fills the room, the house, the town, the state, the country and the world. Know you are love. Know you are divine. Spread your wings. You are special and so are those around you. You can *choose* to share your Divine love with everyone you meet. **Feel Love.**

DIVINE SPARKS

Stand in Your Full Power. You are not a Victim.

What does 'full power' mean to you? Does it mean not allowing yourself to be affected by others' words and actions? Does it mean achieving that which you desire? Through your powers of focus, concentration and strength there is nothing that you cannot achieve and accomplish for yourself.

A victim is one who feels misunderstood and undergoes difficulty, and feels they are made to suffer. You were not put on earth to suffer, undergo difficulty or be misunderstood, although you can choose to have these experiences. Imagine a crossroads: one path is fear and one path is love. On the path of fear you will experience being taken advantage of, cheated, betrayed, deceived and mislead. On the path of love you will experience affection, devotion, kindness, appreciation, intimacy, power and passion.

Become aware of each moment and see if you choose love or fear. Also, there is power in words. When you say I *have to* or I *need to* do something, that gives your power away. When you say **I choose** to, you are in your power. Right now, say those words and feel how it affects your body. Stand in your full power. Become aware and choose love today.

SURRENDER.

Become Fully Who You Are.

Do you yield to your higher power? Are you complete and whole? Surrender and become fully who you are. Be mindful of what you're thinking, saying and doing because it will produce an understanding of yourself. Life does not have to be a struggle. Struggle is what you are creating. In each moment you are creating what you want your future to be through your thoughts, words and actions. To be is to be Divine.

Do you hand over your problems or difficulties to the Divine? If not, why not? Surrender and become fully who you are. The Divine wants to solve your problems and difficulties through faith and trust. Do you worry about your future and feel regret over the past? Past experiences that no longer serve you can be released into love and light. Think of the energy you are using. Become whole.

Remember, there is effort required on your part to take action. Become aware of self. When you no longer like where you are, you are then ready to surrender and hand over your life to the Divine. When surrendering, draw upon your faith and trust—faith and trust to know all is well. The Divine is always there for you. You can *choose* to surrender and become fully who you are.

You can choose to open your heart and yield to the Divine. Free yourself from pain and limitations. Free yourself from resentments and judgments. The Divine is always with you; ask that you may feel comfort by releasing and forgiving. Choose to be open to new ideas, and stay out of opinions about right and wrong, good or bad. View your experience as an experience. Forgive yourself. If you see it as "it just is", you will be living closer to the Divine.

When you decide you no longer want to allow past situations to consume your daily life, then you will be ready to surrender, release and forgive with the help of the Divine. Become responsible for your thoughts and experiences by being aware of what you think and feel moment by moment. This will change the way you live.

As we forgive ourselves and others, our hearts open to love and that love is spread out into the world. Life is what you make it. It is up to you to make the *choice* to stop remembering the past. Focus on the now and create new experiences in your life. Surrender to the moment, release the past and forgive yourself and others through love.

Take a Deep Breath and RELAX.

Say something Positive about YOURSELF!

You can *choose* to slow down, stop and feel your breath. This doesn't sound difficult and it really isn't. However, many of us don't take the time to relax. Are you getting caught up in the physical world, running here, doing that? What about all your obligations and responsibilities? Do you have enough time for everything?

Begin to prioritize your life. Is health important? Is mental clarity important? Is spirituality important? Without a healthy body you do not operate very well, and may feel sluggish, tired or stressed out. Without mental clarity and balance, it is not easy to hear your inner voice and therefore you may have difficult lessons rather than being in the flow. Without connection to Spirit you might feel empty or not satisfied. Take time to relax daily or walk in nature.

Do you think you are unlovable? Do you criticize yourself? Do you think you are a failure? Notice when you are negative about yourself or when you fill your mind with positive thoughts. Become aware. Affirm your positive traits. Know you can be creative. Know you can succeed and accomplish. Know your talents and abilities. *Choose* to think and talk positively.

Take Pressure off Yourself.

ALLOW Situations to Unfold.

Do you feel a heaviness or weight upon your shoulders? Do you feel stress or tension? Do you feel worried or anxious? **STOP.** Take pressure off yourself by relaxing with a deep breath. Close your eyes and smile. Smile and allow beautiful thoughts to fill your mind. At this moment give yourself permission to turn your situation over to your angels, Higher Self, spirit guides or the Divine. Once you have made the decision to do so, forget it. Enjoy today.

Pressure is created by our words. Replace words like *I have to* or *I need to* with *I choose to*. Know all is in the divine plan. If you have completed all you can on this physical level, the rest is up to the universe. Be open to receive. Spirit will reveal the next step.

Listen to your intuition and Spirit will make known what is best. Allow the situations to unfold. Become aware of your thoughts, feelings and guidance. Life is unfolding. Listen to your Higher Self. Imagine your guardian angel watching over you, protecting, loving and supporting you. Feel blessed. Feel the Divine! There is no pressure on you to do or not to do. Feel the power within. Within you is peace. Allow the situations to unfold.

TAKE RESPONSIBILITY.

Your Thoughts are Creating YOUR Reality.

Are you aware of where your thoughts are? Are they in the past, in the future, or in this moment? Become aware of what you are thinking and saying to yourself. If most of the day your thoughts are in the past regretting, feeling guilty, wishing you had or had not done something, how does this serve you? Are your thoughts going to change the past? Have you learned something from the situation? If so, give thanks and release it into love and light.

Are you worried about the future? The future is not here yet, but your thoughts today can help create the type of future you want. Take positive action today for your tomorrow. Take responsibility for your thoughts because they create your reality.

What do you say to yourself first thing in the morning? Is it positive or negative? Are you thankful for a good night's rest? Are you grateful you woke up and you're alive? Start the day out by being in gratitude. Imagine wonderful and delightful things happening. Do you allow others to change your positive attitude? If so, why? You are at choice to focus on the negative or focus on the positive. Be responsible for your thoughts, and create what you desire.

TAKE THE STEP. TRUST & HAVE FAITH.

Take the step. Step into trust. Trust in a higher power. Higher power knows. Know within you, you have the faith. Faith is taking the step. With this the cycle continues. Life is full of unknowns and mysteries. If you feel something is missing in your life, go within and ask for a message. Spirit is always available and will assist you every step you take. Wake up and listen to the voice within.

What do you desire to do? What talent have you not used? Be who you truly are: unlimited in helping and serving yourself and humanity. Once you make the decision to have faith and confidence in your higher power, life is enriched. When you decide to trust your inner guidance and take the step, opportunities open up. Changes begin to happen and life flows more easily. Listen, and take a step into the unknown. Accomplish it! Create it! Go for it!

Have faith that Spirit is working with you to create what is best for your highest good and will. Imagine climbing a ladder that you've checked for loose or broken rungs and now you feel safe to climb. Do the same with Spirit. Check within, feel safe, then take the step. Trust and have faith.

Take Time For Your Own Inner Work.

What gets priority in your life during a 24-hour period? Is there a balance between work, play, family, sleep, and time for yourself? If you are spending 12 hours at work, are you out of balance? Do you feel stress and tension in your body? Are you mentally exhausted? If so, maybe it is time for a change.

Take 10-15 minutes a day for yourself to relax, breathe and give thanks. You will improve physically, mentally and emotionally. Do you sleep 5, 7, or 9 hours at night? Is how much you sleep a habit, or what your body requires? When you spend too much time doing one thing, whether it is working, sleeping, or socializing, it creates an imbalance. It is important to take the time for your spiritual self. Listen. Meditate. Relax the body. Tune into yourself periodically throughout the day. If you are not one to meditate, relax or sit still, then just become aware of moments between activities.

Feel your breath. Taking time for yourself creates a more powerful you. Become aware of how you spend your day. Is it out of habit or from choices? By taking time for your own inner work, you become more productive and in touch with your inner guidance.

The Door to Unconditional LOVE is FORGIVENESS.

What stops you from loving? What conditions have to be met before you love? Where does forgiveness fit into love? What if forgiveness required you to pardon yourself and others now, and free yourself from the past? Would you do it? What words and feelings would it take for you to forgive yourself for all that has happened in the past?

Once you have forgiven yourself and others you no longer think of the past as negative—you see it as a gift and lesson. At that point you choose to move forward into new experiences. By replaying in your mind negative past experiences, you lose precious moments of today's experience. The past is over. You cannot change it, but you do have the power to change today's actions, thoughts and words.

You have the strength to see what is positive. Through visualization and positive thinking you are creating the stage for tomorrow. When fear arises, ask for guidance. Choose love and forgive. Become responsible for your thoughts, words and deeds. Today is fresh and new. Begin to make conscious choices. Forgive yourself, you deserve it! Forgive others, they deserve it! Through love we inspire others to love and forgive.

The
Impossible
is Possible.

If you believe something is unattainable, you're creating it to be unattainable. If you think you can't—you can't. If you think you can—you can. Angels, spirits and guides are ready to help you on your path. You have an unlimited supply of encouragement, direction and wisdom within you. Whenever you desire advice, a Spirit is there to lead. Whenever you want a companion, an angel is there to comfort you. Whenever you are ready for a mentor, one will be there. You are not on this path alone.

Our thoughts create our reality. Are your thoughts of abundance, or lack of it? When you feel hopeless that is what you get, hopelessness. When you believe beyond all the bounds of possibility, beyond the realm of reason, and beyond your own power, and have faith that all is in Divine order, that's when you will be creating. The impossible is possible.

Ask yourself, "Do I deserve the best?" If not, why not? What have you been taught that doesn't allow you to be worthy to receive? Within you are all the ingredients for success, abundance and love. You have the *choice* to change your thinking, which will change your life. It is within your reach; reach for it. The impossible is possible.

The World is your School and Playground. So Have Fun, Learn and Just Be.

What if you came to earth to gain knowledge through experiences? What if your choice before coming to earth was to focus on being independent, having courage and a strong will? You may create certain circumstances and situations that help you to have a greater understanding of independence and courage. You could discover your spiritual self and awaken to that wisdom within by using your intuition to realize your potential. Would that not be school for you?

By being mindful of everyday activities you could have fun in the discovery of self. That is where the playground is. Remember sitting in school learning and creating, and suddenly the bell rings and everyone goes out to play?

The fresh air, sun and dirt was nature's way of re-energizing us for the next lesson. Physical activity is great for our bodies. This is an important part of life: to laugh and be joyful. Life does not have to be so serious. Make a point to have fun, even if it's only briefly. Play creates laughter. Enjoy nature. Each day can be an adventure to have fun, learn and Just Be.

> **TRUST in your Inner Guidance. ACT upon that which You Know.**

Do you depend upon your Higher Self or Divine Guidance? Do you have confidence in a Higher Source? What are your beliefs about God, Higher Self, Divine Consciousness and Universal Mind? Is each one different or are they all the same? Do you practice faith and trust in the unknown? To trust is to place your confidence in something. Trust is something you can depend on. To trust is not to worry.

Sometimes you make choices that are based upon a sense rather than facts. These are times when you **just know**, and it is then that you are listening and trusting in your inner guidance. Each of us is learning, growing and gaining a greater awareness. In every moment you decide to trust in your guidance, or to be in fear. Each time you become aware of making a choice based upon a **knowing,** give thanks. That will strengthen the connection between your higher and lower self.

Only you know what is best for you, not society, parents or friends. How often have you done something that another person suggested and knew it was not the best choice? You have all the answers within you. Act upon that which you know.

TRUST The Voice
'LISTEN'
Deep Within.

Do you believe in a higher power? Would you trust in a higher power? Your guidance and your intuition are within you. To **trust** that guidance and your inner voice is permitting yourself to do something, no matter what others might say. Listen and allow your confidence and strength to surface and then face any situation, difficulty or problem.

Our mind wants to play it safe and says things like, "What if?, Should I?, or Could I?" When that happens, stop that voice and become still. Listen to that knowing. You have all the answers; trust that. By *listening* to that knowing, you are more in the flow of life. Flow of life means you move steadily and continuously, just like water going around rocks.

Do you take time to listen? If not, why not? Too often we get caught up in our daily routine of phones calls, children, work, and other obligations and do not become still. When you first wake up, give thanks for the night and the opportunity for another day. Ask that you be in touch with your guidance throughout the day, and listen for the voice within. Trust yourself and life will present many opportunities.

Understand and the fear will disappear.

As we begin to perceive and accept a person for who they are or a situation for what it is, fear dissipates. Ask yourself questions such as: What am I afraid of? What does this say to me about me? What is the truth?

Take time to understand and come from a place of love. To understand why the fear is there helps to release the fear. The more you understand your and others' experiences, disappointments, hurts, frustrations and successes, the more you open your heart to who you and they are.

With any situation that bothers you, **stop** for a moment and look at all angles and different viewpoints. Step back and see from the eyes of an angel, observing what is going on. Validate all that you see. If you have fear about new beginnings, new relationships or financial difficulties ask yourself, "Do I believe in a higher power? Would I be willing to turn it over to the Divine?" Ask your angels and spirits to be with you. You cannot be in fear and love at the same time. Fear is negative, love is positive. Understand and visualize a place of acceptance, love and peace.

USE COMPASSION in your Present Situation.

Who couldn't use empathy right now? Perhaps a friend, family member, spouse or even you? Compassion is a deep feeling of sharing the suffering of another, a desire to give aid or to show mercy.

When you find yourself in a situation where there is indifference or conflict, are you showing compassion to others and yourself? Is it time for compassion in one of your situations? If so, then do something different, because if you keep doing what you are doing, you will keep getting what you are getting. Come from your heart and act in a new way. Remember, when you change, others change. You can be the example of love rather than hate.

What are you feeling now: hurt, disappointment or guilt? Or are you feeling joyful, loving and grateful? If not, forgive and love yourself. Use compassion. Today show tenderness to someone who annoys you. Be gentle with others who are irritated. Express concern for those having difficulties. Be kindhearted to every individual. You are love and light; know it and believe it. Ask your angels and guides to assist you with thoughts, words and actions for compassion in your present situation.

Use Gentleness and Compassion.

STOP pushing so hard for others to CHANGE.

Do you feel sympathy for others' misfortune? Can you stand where they stand and feel what they feel? Do you understand why they do what they do? Why they say what they say?

Now think for a moment about how you treat yourself. Are you hard on yourself? Do you have expectations or belief systems about how things *should* be? When you are harsh with yourself it shows up as stress in your body. When you push for a specific result rather than allowing life to unfold, life becomes a struggle. Be patient, kind and considerate to yourself. You do not have to be a taskmaster. Be aware of voices that are demanding, over-critical, discounting or harsh and in that moment say 'thank you'. Then replace it with I *choose* to allow, I *choose* to be patient, I *choose* to be grateful, I *choose* to forgive, I *choose* to accept, or whatever would be appropriate.

You cannot change anyone but yourself. Others change when you change. It works. Love yourself through compassion. You are a gift to others, just as they are to you. Use gentleness. Just for today, observe your thoughts, your tone of voice, and how you act and react. Give thanks for your awareness.

Use Gentleness to Touch the Hearts and Minds of others.

Are you gentle with yourself? Do you have negative thoughts that put you down or a critical voice telling you that you are not good enough, not smart enough, not talented enough? Are you confident?

Many times when you are hard on yourself you react that way to others, for what is within is reflected to the outer world. Make a decision to be compassionate and thoughtful towards yourself. Become aware of your tone of voice, words and thoughts about yourself and others. You can make a difference in your life by observing what you do. Notice when you approve or disapprove of yourself. At what point do you love or discount yourself? By answering these questions you have a greater insight and that helps to bring on change for the better.

Visualize yourself being gentle and loving and see that spread out into the universe. Today, use gentleness in every way and watch how you touch the hearts and minds of others. Being kind and considerate is a *choice*. What a gift you are. You deserve to be treated with love; receive from your angles and *feel* love and appreciation. Take this moment to experience the Divine Love. Smile and go forth with gentleness.

Use Intent Toward Your Spiritual Growth.

This book came into your hands for a reason. Your intention toward your own spiritual growth is increasing. Maybe you wish to have a greater understanding of yourself; honor that. You have the power to decide. What do you yearn for in this life? Are you in touch with your purpose? Is there a driving force to know and learn about spirituality? How much time do you give yourself for spiritual growth? Ask yourself these questions and listen.

You are not just this physical body; you are a vast spiritual being living in a small container. You are unlimited. Take this moment and give thanks for the desire to learn more. Determine the priorities in your life: family, friends, career, health, politics or spirituality. Every moment can be a decision for greater awareness.

No matter who you are with or what you are doing, use intent to become aware of thoughts, actions, habits, reactions and tone of voice. Religious and spiritual teachers throughout the ages have talked about living in the moment, and that is the key. You learn and grow while being in the moment. Every second of life, you are who you are consciously or unconsciously. ***Choose*** to live in a state of intention and awareness.

> VISUALIZE PEACEFULNESS. FEEL IT AND ALLOW PEACE TO FLOW THROUGH YOU.

What would your life look like if you and everyone you knew lived in harmony, compassion and good will? What if everyone was cooperative and felt oneness? Close your eyes and visualize strangers having compassion for each other, and friends and family all blending with unity. What does that feel like? What would their words and actions sound like? Peace on earth begins with you.

You must be able to visualize what peace looks and feels like. When each individual finds peace, there will be peace on earth. Start by feeling calm, relaxed and in total comfort. Heal yourself first of all fears, angers, disturbances or discomforts. We cannot be in fear and peace at the same time. *Choose* to be in peace rather than in fear. Peace is harmony, cooperation, serenity, unity, comfort, goodwill, fellowship, patience, calmness and silence. Fear is sadness, resentfulness, hurt, anger, distress, unwillingness, conflict, hostility and anxiety.

No matter what is going on now, you can call upon your angels, guides and spirits to help you through your fears. Release all negativity into love and light. Visualize peace and allow it to flow through you.

VISUALIZE YOURSELF

Laughing and Being Joyful.

Form a mental picture of yourself laughing and being joyful. Stay with it a moment, and see how this visualization affects your body. No matter what is happening for you right now, take time for laughter. Take a load off your shoulders and lighten up.

Be in touch with your physical, emotional and mental body. Are you stressed or relaxed? When you ease up on yourself your body will appreciate it. Uplift yourself and others today. Plant seeds of thoughtfulness. Laugh. Give smiles to everyone you meet. Rejoice in the moment. Let there be a song in your heart. Praise others. Thank someone for who they are. Be delighted. Give a gift. Feel contentment. Share success stories. Write a letter of gratitude. Laugh and be joyful. Every day you have opportunities to laugh and be joyful in life.

Create how you want to feel through your thoughts and actions. It is your point of view that sets the stage for your attitude. You can decide to see humor, or be serious. See beauty rather than ugliness. Take positive steps rather than negative ones. If this message is a reminder that you are laughing and being joyful then give thanks for refreshing your memory, and continue on your journey with love.

YOU ARE SURROUNDED BY BEAUTY. EXPERIENCE IT!

No matter where you live, there is beauty. No matter who you are, there is beauty within. No matter where you work, there is beauty in the situation. There is beauty in nature, art, music, people and animals. Beauty is a gift from the Divine Spirit. There is beauty everywhere.

Today, look at the clouds, sky, faces of children, flowers, trees, watch the birds in flight and experience what beauty does for you. Look for the beauty within YOU! Become aware of your thoughts today. Are they filled with love and beauty or filled with worry and regret? Make a *choice* today to see beauty in all things. What are you thankful for? Is there beauty there? Make an effort to view things as if you are seeing them for the first time, and find new beauty within.

There are thousands of thoughts and images that you can create today to beautify your world. There are thousands of words you can say to others to beautify their world. There are thousands of actions you can take to create beauty in the world. Decide to experience beauty today. Remember, beauty brings forth love. Love creates joy. Experience it!

You are the Creator of your Reality.

SMILE

Reality is the state or quality of being real. What type of environment do you desire for yourself: loving, nourishing, cooperative, confident, giving? What are you doing today to plant the seeds for tomorrow's growth? What you sow is what you reap. Are you spreading seeds of fruitful harvest or seeds of destruction? Are you tossing positive or negative thoughts into the air? Are you increasing your faith and security or investing in doubts and insecurities?

Choose to think beautiful thoughts and create a feeling of joy through visualization. Throughout the day, give thoughts of love to everyone you meet. See yourself as abundant and happy. Be delighted for others' success and prosperity. See yourself as successful. Take pleasure in others' achievements. There is an inexhaustible supply of love, joy and peace for everyone. Tap into yours.

You can be an example. You can create the state of being you desire through your *choice* of words, thoughts and actions. Each of us creates our own reality. Smile and love so others may see your light. You are the creator of your reality.

YOU CAN OVERCOME ANYTHING.

ALL IS WELL!

No matter what is happening right now, Spirit is with you. No matter what you are thinking, Spirit is with you. All is in divine order for you to learn from your experiences. Believe the situation is part of a divine plan and know this is an opportunity to prevail.

Call upon your angels to comfort you. Call upon your Higher Self to guide you. Ask your Spirit guides to relieve you of any stress and lighten your burdens. When you worry over finances, you are saying to the universe, "I am fearful there is not enough." Your thoughts create your reality. Instead of *choosing* to worry, think abundant, see yourself abundant, act abundant and feel abundant. Thank the universe right now for all you have. By focusing on assets rather than lack, you can create a feeling of abundance. You can overcome anything.

Do you want a wonderful relationship? Imagine what it would look and feel like. How would you act? What would you say to each other? What feelings would you have? Know you can create it. Let it flow. Want a wonderful career? Imagine it and create it. You are powerful within; overcome. Start visualizing what you want. Know all is well.

You have
the
Courage
to
Complete.

DETERMINATION.

What in your life is not complete? What is left undone? Is there something unfinished you have energy on? Where are your thoughts during the day, in the past or future? Draw upon your inner strength to face obstacles and tribulations in your life.

Ask yourself, "What is the worst that can happen in this situation?" How would you deal with it? Who would you call upon for help? Take a moment and become still. Ask your guardian angel, spirit guides, and the Divine what is best for you at this time. Stay out of judgment about what you hear; just listen. When you do what others or society thinks is best instead of following your own inner guidance, you give your power away. You have the knowingness within. Once you arrive at a decision you can be at peace. Energy is wasted by being confused, worried or unsettled.

Today, take action. Move in the direction you want to go. Accomplish, achieve, terminate, wrap up, realize or resolve what is left undone. Decide what is best. Do it. Being aware of your spiritual side allows you to develop into an enriched, complete and fine-tuned person. Listen and know. Tell yourself you have the courage to complete through determination.

ABOUT THE AUTHOR

Shelia Shumate is an author, motivational speaker, and intuitive counselor. She has presented  workshops and seminars on communication and self-awareness since 1985, and has also volunteered hundreds of hours in self-consciousness training.

Shelia has been a practicing intuitive counselor for many years. She brings in Divine Guidance in her sessions,

SHELIA SHUMATE

helping to heal and empower others.

Shelia is the owner of Just Be Creations in Sedona, Arizona, that makes inspirational items. To find out more about her work and to read inspirational messages, visit her website at www.JustBe Creations.com.